Fraver BY DESIGN

5 DECADES
OF THEATRE POSTER ART FROM
BROADWAY,
OFF-BROADWAY,
AND BEYOND

FRANK "FRAVER" VERLIZZO

Schiffer Publishing Ltd

4880 Lower Valley Road • Atglen, PA 19310

Other Schiffer Books on Related Subjects:
*Alternative Movie Posters II: More Film Art
from the Underground*, Matthew Chojnacki,
978-0-7643-4986-7

Hollywood Movie Posters: 1914–1990,
Miles Barton, 978-0-7643-2010-1

*Movie Posters: 75 Years of Academy® Award
Winners*, Diana DiFranco Everett and Morris
Everett Jr., 978-0-7643-1789-7

Book Cover Designs, Matthew Goodman,
978-0-7643-5016-0

Type set in Minion Pro/Helvetica Neue LT Pro

ISBN: 978-0-7643-5515-8
Printed in China

Published by Schiffer Publishing, Ltd.
4880 Lower Valley Road
Atglen, PA 19310
Phone: (610) 593-1777; Fax: (610) 593-2002
E-mail: Info@schifferbooks.com
Web: www.schifferbooks.com

For our complete selection of fine books on this
and related subjects, please visit our website at
www.schifferbooks.com. You may also write for
a free catalog.

Schiffer Publishing's titles are available at
special discounts for bulk purchases for sales
promotions or premiums. Special editions,
including personalized covers, corporate
imprints, and excerpts, can be created in
large quantities for special needs. For more
information, contact the publisher.

We are always looking for people to write
books on new and related subjects. If you
have an idea for a book, please contact us
at proposals@schifferbooks.com.

Dedicated to Joseph Ligammari,
for making every day since 1977
a fun adventure; and my mother,
Nancy, who would have
loved this book.

CONTENTS

PREFACE

I am thrilled that Frank is documenting his work via this extraordinary book.

The New York Public Library for the Performing Arts at Lincoln Center was so proud to present a vast array of his beautiful posters in *Design: Fraver* in 2011. It was a very popular exhibit—more than 30,000 people had a chance to view the exhibit each month. I was thrilled to think of the thousands of visitors who had seen it, and felt sad that others might have missed it when it came down. With this book, we all have the opportunity to celebrate the work of this exceptionally talented artist. I will treasure my copy.

I urge you to choose a favorite or two out of the hundreds of images within. It was impossible for me. Every one of the posters created for Broadway and Off-Broadway, as well as regional theatre and beyond, is outstanding. You simply have to savor them all. Happy reading.

– Jacqueline Z. Davis, Executive Director of the New York Public Library for the Performing Arts at Lincoln Center

SUNDAY in the PARK with GEORGE

A Musical

The Shubert Organization and Emanuel Azenberg
by arrangement with
Playwrights Horizons
present

Mandy   Bernadette
Patinkin   Peters

in

SUNDAY in the PARK with GEORGE
A Musical

Music and Lyrics by
Stephen Sondheim

Book by
James Lapine

Scenery by	Costumes by		Lighting by
Tony	Patricia	Ann	Richard
Straiges	Zipprodt and Hould-Ward		Nelson

Special Effects by	Sound by	Hair and Makeup
Bran Ferren	Tom Morse	Lo Presto/Allen

Musical Direction by	Orchestrations by	Movement by
Paul	Michael	Randolyn
Gemignani	Starobin	Zinn

Directed by
James Lapine

⑤ Booth Theatre 45th Street West of Broadway

FOREWORD

DAVID EDWARD BYRD
ILLUSTRATOR

In early 1971, as a freelance illustrator working in New York City, I had designed two Broadway theatre posters that were attracting some attention: Stephen Sondheim's *Follies* and Stephen Schwartz's *Godspell*. This lucky theatrical confluence led to my being asked to teach a class in beginning illustration at Pratt Institute in Brooklyn.

I had never taught an art class before, but I was known to blabber on a bit so I figured I could wing it. This very first class of my teaching career had a certain magical abundance of young talent. One strapping fellow stood out; his name was Frank Verlizzo. His class projects often revealed to me a very modern sensibility, a lively imagination, and, best of all, a wicked sense of humor.

At the time of that first class, I had only been creating posters for three years. I was myself a novice, but I believed that a poster should be calling to you from across the street, luring you in, or punching you in the face. But the theatre posters of that day had so many credits in so many sizes that there was little room for art: for example, a show called *Bazoom* would have the title loosely lettered with a busty woman popping out of one of the "Os"—that was it! (Boring.)

Frank Verlizzo could never be boring—he liked big images with flair, verve, and pizzazz. That is why I recommended him to Morris Robbins, the indefatigable art director of Blaine Thompson, the biggest theatrical advertising agency of the day. He was immediately hired and became their stellar artist in no time at all, adding poster after poster to his portfolio.

As the cliché goes, the rest is history and Fraver is now undoubtedly the "Poster King of the Great Rialto." He has created more theatre posters than any person living or dead, I am sure. It is the dream of any art teacher that a student might become a great success as an artist. Frank Verlizzo has made this teacher's dream come true. I am surely blessed.

ACKNOWLEDGMENTS

Hawley Abelow
Gerard Alessandrini
The American Theatre
    Wing
Bryan Andes
Emanuel Azenberg
Lani Azenberg
Laney Katz Becker
Leah Becker
Hugh Beeson Jr.
Rob Berman
Sue Ellen Beryl
Jon Bierman
Jared Bradshaw
The Broadway League
Craig D. Burke
David Edward Byrd
Liz Callaway
Ted Chapin
Peter Chenot
Sherri Cohen
Jacqueline Z. Davis
John DiMaio
Disney Theatrical
    Group
Jean Doumanian
Kenn Duncan
T Charles Erickson
Elizabeth Findlay
Bert Fink
Angelina Fiordellisi
Andrew Flatt

Dan Foster
John Freedson
Paul Gaschler
Aaron Grant
Ralph & Calla Guild
Jean-Marie Guyaux
Bill Haber
Tex Hauser
William Hayes
Adam Hess
Heather A. Hitchens
Judy Katz
Judy Kaye
Annie Keefe
Douglas Kirkland
David J. Kitto
Paul Kolnik
Meri Krassner
Mark Lamos
Joseph Ligammari
Jeff Lilley
Scott Lupi
Aaron Lustbader
Ivan Mair
Catherine Major
Joan Marcus
Jesse Marth
Carey Massimini
Walter McBride
Rick Miramontez
Scott Morfee
Thomas Mygatt

Amin Osman
Joey Parnes
Bernadette Peters
Dean Pitchford
John Reilly
Doug Reside
Julie Richards
Debra Robbins
Carol Rosegg
Diane Rosner
Daryl Roth
Susan L. Schulman
Mark Shacket
Claudia Shear
Dana Siegel
Bruce Simons
Leida Snow
Frederick Speers
Danielle Poncheri
    Speicher
Charlotte St. Martin
Jean Stone
Seth Stuhl
Cassandra Summer
Martha Swope
Gasper Tringale
Anne Trites
Triton Gallery
Nick van Hoogstraten
Jack Viertel
Jessica L. White
Max Woodward

INTRODUCTION

Art isn't easy.

– Stephen Sondheim, *Sunday in the Park with George*

As a Manhattan-born teenager at the High School of Art and Design on East 57th Street, I was starstruck and practically lived at the movies. I once raced through an end of term French exam in order to catch the early afternoon showing of *Boom!* playing down the street at the late, great Sutton Cinema. My big dream didn't involve acting or directing, but designing the poster art for films. I have vivid memories of watching the billboard artwork for the Twentieth Century Fox epic *Cleopatra* being painted by men on scaffolds at the palatial Rivoli Theatre on Broadway. As an art student, I had no frame of reference as to how or where the existing poster art plastered around the city was created and produced. But I knew I wanted to find out and become a part of it.

Fast forward about thirty years or so. I'm standing once again on Broadway watching a huge billboard facade being installed, not for the Queen of Egypt, but for *The Lion King*. Along with the artwork I've created for other great Broadway classics, including *Sweeney Todd, Deathtrap,* and *Sunday in the Park with George*, I am now watching my own designs contribute to the visual grandeur of Times Square. My job as a graphic artist specializing in theatre posters is to create a two-dimensional representation of a show, be it play or musical. I must distill a two-and-a-half-hour stage production into an image that is memorable and eye-catching, but most of all serves as an effective selling tool. All of that while hopefully possessing the attributes of a frame-worthy piece of artwork that will hang in homes, schools, and regional theatres across America, and in some cases, the world.

Fate was kind to me in my career pursuit. I majored in advertising and illustration at Brooklyn's Pratt Institute. Senior year, my teacher was legendary poster artist David Edward Byrd. David's work for the Fillmore East rock concerts was famous. He was responsible for ushering into the art world a new wave by creating bold, graphic, and psychedelic posters for the likes of Jimi Hendrix, Jefferson Airplane, and The Grateful Dead. He was a technical wizard as well in cutting Rubylith film masks and using an airbrush. He held classes in his townhouse just off campus. I remember walking into his studio and seeing taped to his drawing board a work-in-progress for a new Broadway musical.

I do believe David's *Follies* single-handedly revitalized interest in the theatre poster as an art form. Until then, much of it consisted of celebrity headshots accompanied by artistic brush lettering.

Upon graduating, David suggested that I show my work to his art director at Blaine Thompson, New York's premiere theatrical advertising agency. My portfolio pretty much consisted of the posters I had designed for David's class. They were all movie oriented—*Crawford* being a typical example of an illustration I created for class. I worked primarily in color pencil and acrylic paint. For black and white illustrations I used a standard yellow number two graphite pencil.

The art director and head designer, Morris Robbins, must have liked what he saw. He offered me a freelance assignment for an upcoming musical, *The Andrews Sisters in Over Here!* I was both excited and disappointed in that I was really looking for full-time employment.

I learned a rather harsh reality lesson from working on that first show. Morris explained that although the producers loved parts of my posters, it was asked that the favored elements be applied to a poster already pretty much approved but created by another artist. As consolation, however, he asked that I submit my portfolio for another upcoming Broadway project.

The request of that client to the agency was to collect as many artists' portfolio samples as possible from which they'd select three to create poster comps for their show. A week later, Morris called and excitedly told me that out of all those portfolios, the artists that the producers selected were David Byrd, Hilary Knight (from Eloise fame), and myself! The show was the revival of *Gypsy* starring Angela Lansbury. I thought that was a really nice consolation prize indeed!

Hilary Knight's poster was chosen and, unfortunately, my *Gypsy* poster comp has long since disappeared. Working on that show did give me entry to the agency. Months later, Morris called and offered me a full-time job in the art department of Blaine Thompson. It was made clear that I was being hired to do production. That entailed designing layouts for newspaper ads, billboards, marquees, and flyers for every show the agency handled. Of course, each show had its own key art created by a variety of illustrators and photographers, but it enabled me to meet and talk with the best in the business on Broadway.

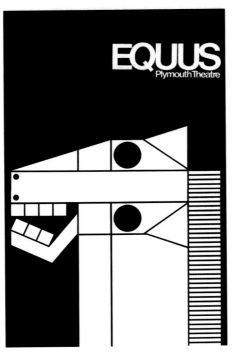

Courtesy of David Edward Byrd   Courtesy of the author ©Gilbert Lesser   Courtesy of Debra Robbins

As one of several artists in the production department, I learned the process of creating poster art and building an ad campaign for a new show. I very much wanted to sit in on client presentations to see how they worked, but that was reserved for the art directors. My "day job" was in the production department, but after six o'clock, I had access to all the scripts of upcoming shows, as well as everything I needed to create poster comps—I was free to design.

Morris was a most wonderful first boss as well as being incredibly talented and humble about it all. He was responsible for creating some of the most memorable logo designs in Broadway history: the graphic icon for *Funny Girl*, the original *How to Succeed in Business Without Really Trying*, and the premiere artwork for *Hello, Dolly!* among so many others. He was a tremendous influence on how I approached a project and tutored me in the reality of illustration versus graphics. He also taught me how to work gracefully under pressure, probably the most important lesson of all.

Generally, once I had a strong concept, it would take three or four evenings' work in order to sketch it out and paint it. On one occasion, Morris suggested that I treat my concept as a graphic rather than a full-blown illustration. I took his advice and found that simplifying my image allowed me to create several of my ideas in the same time that all that painting took. I soon discovered that I loved graphics as much as I loved illustration.

Another major influence was meeting graphic designer Gilbert Lesser. Morris introduced us during the run of *Equus*. Gil had created the powerful graphic that launched the ad campaign. I was fascinated by how he was able to break an idea down to its simplest form and yet give it incredible strength, excitement, and elegance. He created all of his poster comps by cutting or tearing Pantone paper to desired effect. Among so many others, his designs for the Broadway productions of *Frankenstein*, *Rex*, and *The Elephant Man* are extraordinary. My poster for *The Lady and the Clarinet*, starring Stockard Channing, was an homage to him. Whenever he'd visit the art department, he would tell Morris, "Always remember, I taught Fraver how to cut paper!"

I use the name Fraver to sign my posters. At the High School of Art and Design, few teachers could pronounce my last name and I thought it too complex, so I merged the first three letters of my first and last names. By the time I attended David Byrd's first class at Pratt Institute, I had cemented Fraver as my signature.

Fraver

CHAPTER ONE

BROADWAY

My first Broadway poster was for Tom Stoppard's *Travesties*, which went on to win the Best Play Tony Award that year, so it was not a bad start. It was followed by a short-lived prison play, *The Poison Tree*, which was important to me because it was how I began my association with producer Emanuel Azenberg, who was an admirer of my work. He requested that the agency have me design posters for many of his productions, with *Sunday in the Park with George* being the ultimate example. I believe it was my graphic for the original production of David Mamet's *American Buffalo,* followed by my poster for Ira Levin's hit thriller, *Deathtrap*, that led me to be moved out of the Blaine Thompson production department and into a small office of my own about ten feet away.

I was now an assistant art director and permitted to design posters every day as part of my job. I was in heaven!

Nothing lasts forever, of course, and after about another year of first job bliss, Blaine Thompson closed its doors. This paved the way for other theatrical ad agencies to open and flourish. All of them were pretty much comprised of the folks who had worked at BT. I was employed by many of them at various times: J. Walter Thompson Entertainment Group; Serino, Coyne & Nappi; LeDonne, Wilner & Weiner; Grey Entertainment; Rave! Advertising; and Eliran Murphy Group. Each agency had a distinct personality and I enjoyed working at every one of them. As you read the behind-the-scenes stories of each poster you are about to see, you'll learn a bit more about these agencies and the process of creating printed art for the theatre.

Commentaries by women and men from various aspects of the theatre world are featured in this book. Rather than reading only my version of the poster design process, I thought it would be fascinating for other theatre-related personalities to contribute their thoughts on what posters mean to them. Getting a fresh perspective from the opposite side of the table will always prove interesting. Several of these theatre glitterati were present at my various art presentations, while others will comment on their impressions of the finished products. Many provide a brief background history of our association and the various projects on which we worked together.

You might also be aware that some of the posters are shown in their entirety, with show billing and theatre information. Others are presented as artwork rather than the final printed poster. That was an artistic choice on my part, to focus on the design rather than the advertising. In some instances, a preferred, slightly altered version may be shown rather than the final approved image. Peppered among the chosen poster concepts are sketches and comps that were not selected. They are sometimes fun to observe in retrospect. The segue from working in pre-technology years to the post technology age will also come into play. A lot has happened to influence theatre poster art and its creation in five decades!

Writer Ira Levin had catapulted to fame via his novel *Rosemary's Baby*. The ad agency had a script circulating around the office for his new play, a thriller, entitled *Deathtrap*. I was a major fan of his ever since his brilliant novel *A Kiss Before Dying*. The play was a real page-turner and generated lots of anticipated excitement amongst our group. There was no doubt about it, I was determined to design the poster for this new Broadway play. I must have been completely focused on achieving that goal because I have no recollection of any other artist working on it or any poster submissions, although clearly there must have been several. I grabbed a small office mirror, propped it up on my desk and drew a sinister-looking graphic version of my eyes. At the last minute, I chose to make them bright blue to garner instant attention.

It was a period in theatre history before the advent of direct mail. Every new play or musical opening on Broadway had to rely heavily on its announcement ad in *The New York Times*. The full page ad for *Deathtrap*, as with every other opening ad, featured a coupon at its base to purchase tickets. The customer would fill it out and mail it in to the theatre box office with a check or money order. From initial ad until the coupons started rolling in, there was a lot of breath holding. The price of the top ticket for an orchestra aisle seat was a whopping $17.50.

Stevie Wonder Billboard (1977)

Photography courtesy of the author

Deathtrap was smiled upon by the theatre gods. It received lukewarm to rave reviews, but as any opening night audience member could attest, it was destined to become a big hit. The crowd loved it—genuinely laughing, and screaming with fear in all the right places. It is mind-boggling, looking back, that any play could survive without the benefit of direct mail, not to mention e-mail blasts, which were still twenty years away from theatre application. The likes of Playbill.com, Broadway Box, and TheaterMania were also not a part of the landscape. They didn't yet exist as valuable advertising entities created to prime potential audience members into buying a ticket. Despite all of this, *Deathtrap* ran to packed houses for four years. Now, that's a true Broadway hit!

My favorite Times Square signage no longer exists. The Marriott Hotel and Marquis Theatre now stand in its place on Broadway. The billboard spanned the entire block between 45th and 46th Streets and was hard to miss even in that visually crowded environment. It was typically employed to herald the coming of a monumental film. I remember being awestruck by the *Spartacus* artwork as a kid. Men on scaffolds would hand-paint the entire facade guided by a paper grid. It was a costly investment for any advertising budget. Only major motion pictures seemed to be able to afford it. In 1977, the billboard remained blank for a long time. It was slated to be destroyed to make way for a Broadway hotel.

Meanwhile, on another front, the public was anxiously awaiting Stevie Wonder's new album, *Songs in the Key of Life*. But the release of the record kept getting delayed. Gossip hinted that there was no album. In order to suppress those rumors, the record label decided to make a splashy commitment by renting the costly outdoor space. Publicity pictures of the album cover created by the label had already been released. I was asked simply to create a press kit cover for Stevie Wonder. Using color pencils and acrylics, I went to work. Soon after my artwork was approved, the client requested that I adapt my design and illustration (also to incorporate the existing record cover art) for the block-long billboard. When it was completed, my signature was two feet high on the corner of 46th Street and Broadway. I think I dragged everyone I'd ever met to see it. It was the last time that space was used before demolition.

Travesties (1975)

Soon after I began at Blaine Thompson Advertising, I was very fortunate to have as one of my first projects a prestigious Tom Stoppard show that would go on to win the Tony Award for Best Play. Since I was very new to the business, I wasn't invited to the ad meetings and almost ten years passed before I finally met Broadway legend David Merrick, who was the producer. The only directive given in designing the logo was that it had to be done using Merrick Red, which was a particular shade of his favorite color. King Displays always had at the ready their special paint mixture to be used on the marquees for any Merrick show.

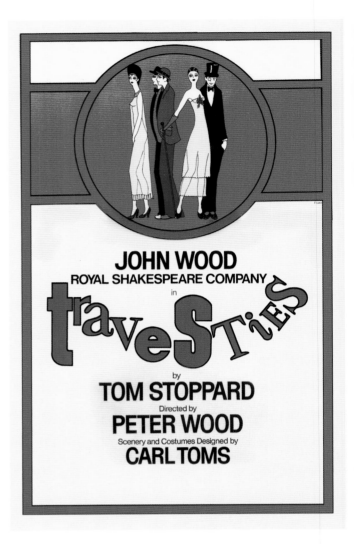

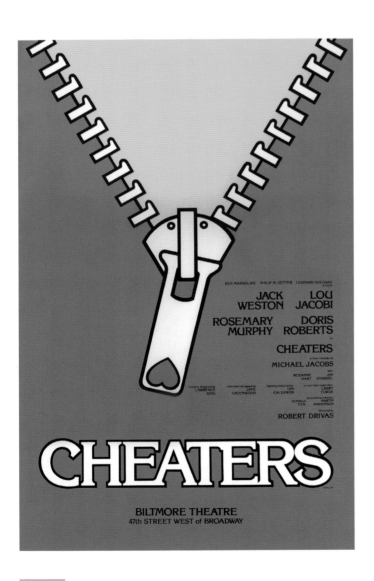

Cheaters (1978)

The show was a huge disaster and closed after thirty-three performances. The most remarkable thing about this poster was that for the many years I lived in Turtle Bay, the parking garage next door had a *Cheaters* one-sheet pasted to its wall. Because of my proximity, I saw my artwork on display every day for years after the show had closed!

American Buffalo (1977)

I had the pleasure of designing posters for two New York City productions of this David Mamet play—the original Broadway production and The Atlantic Theatre Company's presentation twenty-three years later! My idea for the Broadway show was to print the entire nickel image spanning two window cards, with billing on the left-hand card and critic's quotes on the right-hand card. Everyone on the production team loved the idea but it proved financially impossible. I then redesigned the poster using the full nickel on one window card in silver ink on black. Years later, I got the chance to use my two-card idea for Atlantic but once again, for budgetary purposes the idea got nixed, and only the left card was printed!

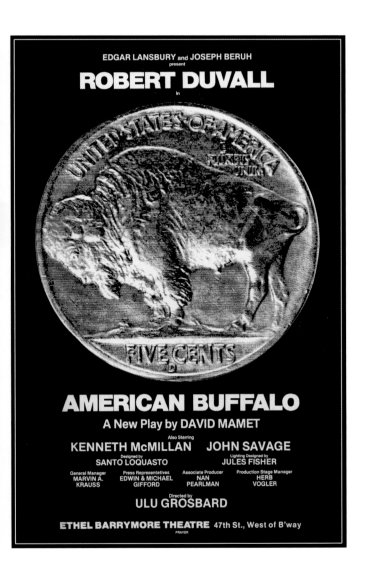

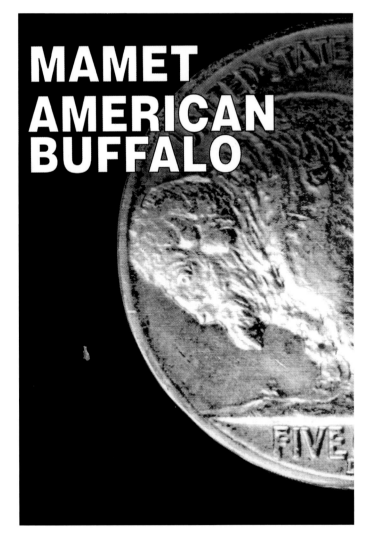

Beyond Therapy (1982)

Every so often a script would capture the imagination of the entire ad agency and *Beyond Therapy* was just such a script. This play certainly made its rounds through the office and it was my first exposure to the writing brilliance of Christopher Durang. Everyone who read it said they did so while laughing—without stopping. We really were expecting it to be Broadway's next long-running comedy hit. I imagined my embryonic cartoon character blazing bright on the Brooks Atkinson Theatre marquee for years. It was my introduction to "what's working on the page may not be working on the stage," despite a terrific cast and playwright. It closed after only twenty-one performances.

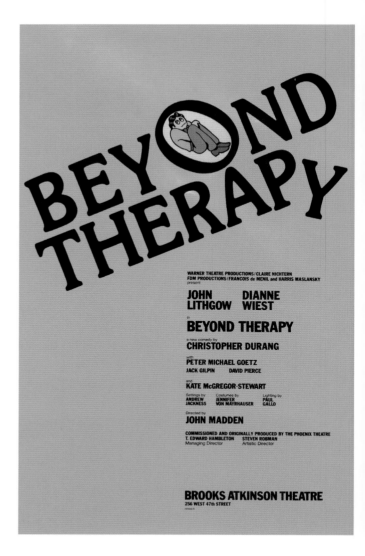

Otherwise Engaged (1977)

Often the simplest solutions are the best ones. In Simon Gray's wonderful play, actor Tom Courtenay portrayed an intellectual whose plan of spending some time listening to his favorite music is interrupted by a series of unexpected visitors. Using a knot as the image seemed a perfect expression of this character's frustrated state of mind. The producers agreed. Early on, I showed my design to my future husband, Joe. When the show opened, he presented me with a custom-made silver knot ring that replicated my poster graphic. I'm certain that in today's marketing-savvy climate, it would be mass-produced and sold in the lobby during intermission.

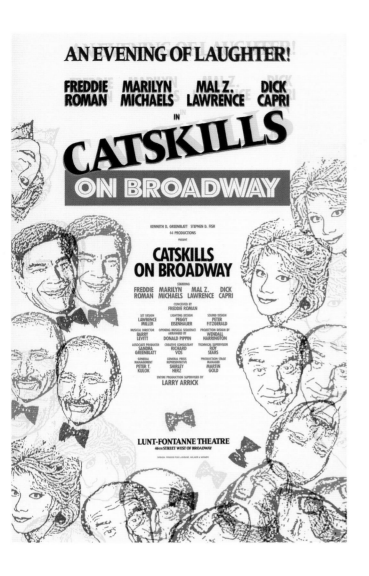

This was definitely the surprise hit of the season, garnering rave reviews, many packed houses, and performers who truly satisfied audiences. I'd never experienced Catskills humor personally but the phrase "riot of color" popped into my head, so I went with it. I used the office copier to give a rough texture to my sketches of the comedians, a device I used quite often before the advent of computer technology. It was an accessible, inexpensive way to treat artwork without having to go to great expense by ordering a screened velox or mezzotint from an outside vendor.

Prymate (2004)

I designed the graphic for this play in tribute to one of my all-time favorite movie poster designers, Saul Bass. He was the man responsible for the ad campaigns for Alfred Hitchcock's *Psycho, Vertigo,* and *North by Northwest,* as well as the films *West Side Story* and *Anatomy of a Murder.* His unique graphic style has been borrowed and reinterpreted countless times. I jumped on the Bass bandwagon in designing for this controversial show. At the presentation, the producing team zeroed in on it right away and no changes were made to the piece.

COMMENTARY
MANNY AZENBERG
THEATRE PRODUCER AND GENERAL MANAGER

If you ask me if I get involved in the creative process, I say no. The creators are the writers, the composers, the painters, and the sculptors. There can only be one painter; the rest of us are framers. Selecting a logo or a design for a new play or musical was always an event loaded with so many other voices, so many unwanted opinions.

We should go to the theatre for a revelation! To see, hear, or experience something new—or in a new way. I do a play if it moves me. First is the visceral reaction. Then comes the intellectual reaction. A theatre poster should reflect that as well.

Fraver's work was always artistic and eloquent. It was a joy to go through this process with him on our shows. He is one of the "creators."

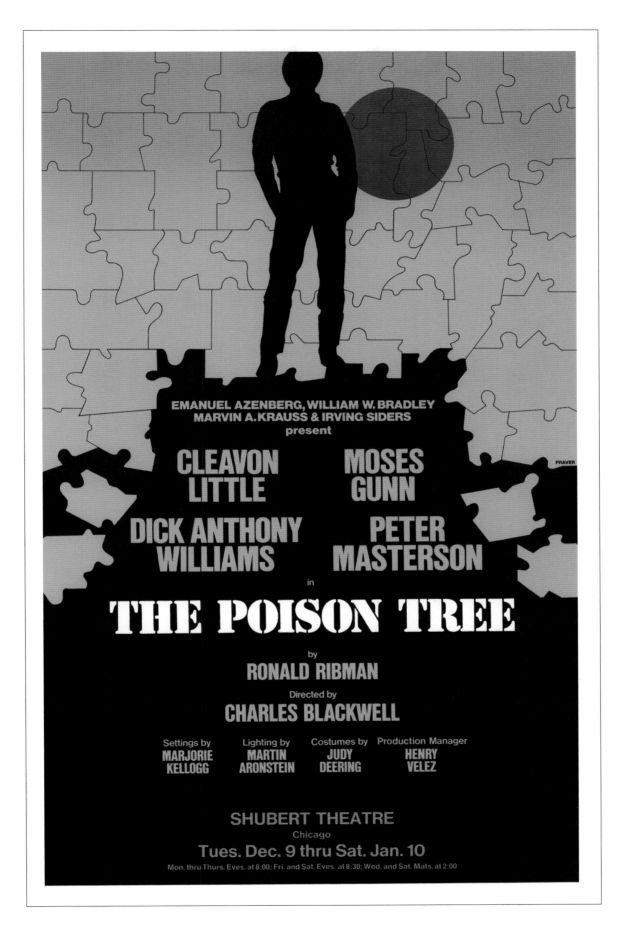

EMANUEL AZENBERG, WILLIAM W. BRADLEY
MARVIN A. KRAUSS & IRVING SIDERS
present

FRAVER

CLEAVON
LITTLE

MOSES
GUNN

DICK ANTHONY
WILLIAMS

PETER
MASTERSON

in

THE POISON TREE

by

RONALD RIBMAN

Directed by

CHARLES BLACKWELL

Settings by	Lighting by	Costumes by	Production Manager
MARJORIE KELLOGG	MARTIN ARONSTEIN	JUDY DEERING	HENRY VELEZ

SHUBERT THEATRE
Chicago
Tues. Dec. 9 thru Sat. Jan. 10
Mon. thru Thurs. Eves. at 8:00; Fri. and Sat. Eves. at 8:30; Wed. and Sat. Mats. at 2:00

Having already had a limited and well-received run at the Hudson Guild Theatre, expectations were high for this play about the survivors of the Donner Party. The story is about a group of pioneers who were trapped in the Sierra Nevada during the brutal winter of 1847. After a harrowing event like that, I felt those mountains were most certainly haunted by those unfortunate early settlers. That gave me the idea for the mountain made of faces. The producers chose the poster right away. However, the theatre-going public clearly found the play's subject matter too extreme. It ran a total of five performances.

It was always big news when a new play by hit-maker-playwright Neil Simon was opening on Broadway. This show was no exception. Working with producer Manny Azenberg, the biggest challenge I faced on the advertising end of things was how much this poster was going to cost to reproduce. I had created it as a line drawing and designed it to be printed in a twelve-color silk-screen process using multi-layered rubyliths designated to represent each color. It's hard to believe in today's world of digital printing, but in 1980 that would have cost a fortune. I had also asked that the postcard image be spot laminated to make it stand out from the creamy white background. The theatre gods were on my side and the poster was printed as designed.

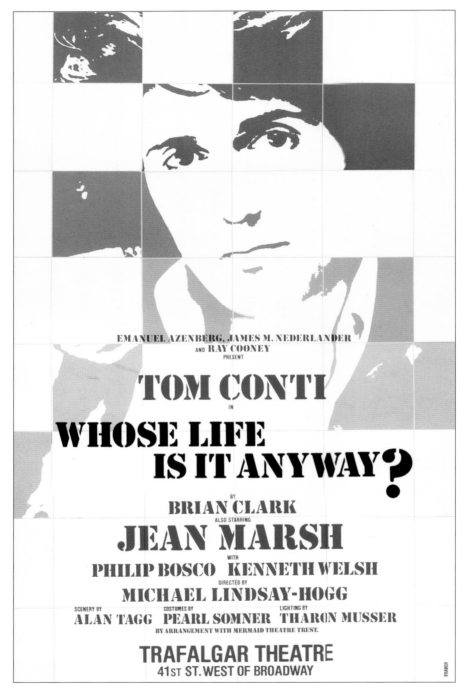

The play is about a patient immobilized in a hospital bed. Producer Manny Azenberg was adamant: the artwork was to look hopeful, upbeat, and not depressing. No medical images of beds, nurses, etc. I agreed with that theory since the play did have much humor and our objective, after all, was to sell tickets to a show, not make it look like an ad for health care. In my design I chose to focus on the white tiles one finds in most hospitals. These blocks were then pieced together to form the portrait of actor Tom Conti. The image was chosen, and in addition to being the poster art, it became our animated television spot, too. The show was a major success and won Mr. Conti a Best Actor Tony Award.

I had already designed the poster for the original Broadway production, starring Tom Conti, a year earlier. Now, producer Manny Azenberg created a media stir by casting Mary Tyler Moore in the role. I followed my format using a graphic portrait of the star and got to meet MTM backstage one day between matinee and evening performances. Her hairstylist, who also cut my hair, told me she wanted to meet the artist. She signed a poster for me with the inscription: "To Frank: Thank you for my face."

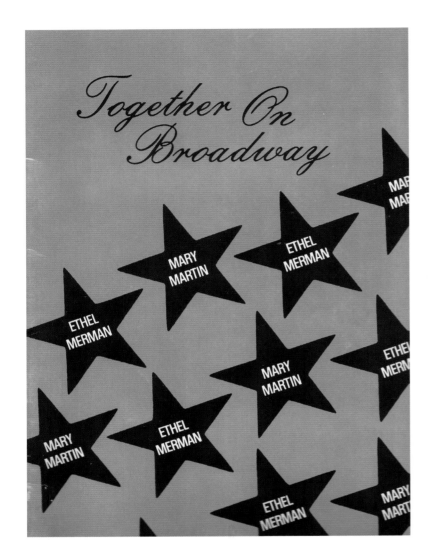

Photography by Jon Bierman

I was still working in the Blaine Thompson art department when I was asked to come up with a design solution to a tricky billing dilemma. Ethel Merman and Mary Martin were giving a special benefit performance for one night only at the Broadway Theatre. They had been rejecting all of the artwork presented because for each piece, one of them didn't like her billing. Whose name would come first? The event was called *Together on Broadway*. I designed a cover that was gold (a no-brainer) with a pattern of stars. On each star was either the name Ethel Merman or Mary Martin. Depending on how you looked at the cover (left to right, top to bottom) the overall effect was that both divas were billed equally. In case that wasn't sufficient, when you flipped the souvenir program to the back cover, the names on the graphic stars alternated in the opposite order as the front. The inside of the book follows suit. One half is all Merman. If you flip the book over, it becomes all Martin. The ladies were very pleased with the design.

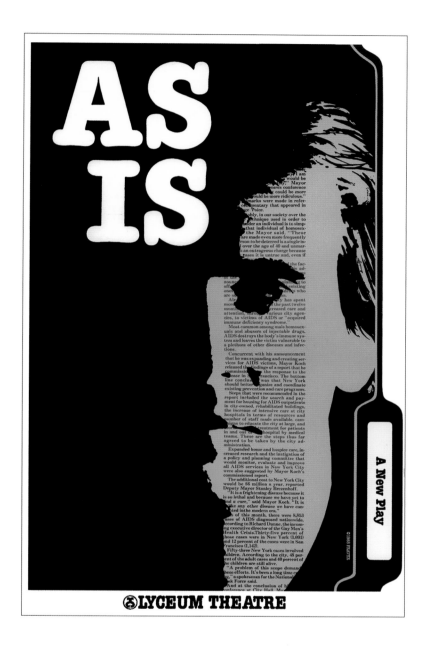

This was producer John Glines's first big Broadway play since *Torch Song Trilogy* and he was very hands on in all aspects of the advertising. My good friend Ivan Mair took the photograph of another friend, Bruce Simons. The picture was meant as a place holder for comp purposes only, since I thought whoever was playing the role would later be photographed. Glines loved the look of it and decided to go with the photograph. When I called Bruce to get permission to use his likeness, I was told he was on vacation for a few weeks. This was back in the days before the ubiquitous cell phone. When people were on vacation, you had to wait for them to return to speak with them! John felt strongly about using the image, and knowing Bruce as well as I did, we went ahead with all the materials. By the time Bruce came back from his holiday, his face was plastered on wild postings all over New York City and in *New York Times* ads. Quite a welcome home! Fortunately, as I suspected, he was thrilled.

It can be love at first sight. That delusion brought about by passion and lust.

A lightning strike of the red Pimpernel color that leaves you breathless. Leaves you wanting more.

Seeking him here, seeking him there, seeking him everywhere. Or perhaps the sullen frightened images of World War I soldiers you may never see again. If only you could reach out and touch them deeply at this very moment.

A poster brings life. That is what theatre and film art posters do. They grab immediately, unexpectedly, passionately. They awaken you!

They jolt you out of your calm, staid life and propel you dangerously into a world and love affair you never expected to share. That is how Frank Verlizzo plays cupid for us all—the Dolly Levi of the Great White Way.

Sometimes, as in Nora Ephron's *Imaginary Friends*, the love affair is doomed, despite the sharpness of the arrow: kept apart by the pedigree and intellect of it all.

But the poster draws you in anyway. That quote about a "bitch" questions the affair in the very beginning. You do pay attention.

That's what brilliant poster art does. Tempts the suitor to fall seriously in love. Pulls him in to an affair, a world aglow. Whether after the first glance, this first date, an endearing match is made, that's beyond even the brilliance of Frank Verlizzo. Or any designer or any poster art.

It is somehow written in the stars, beyond the grasp of mere mortals.

This entertaining show about the famous feud between authors Lillian Hellman and Mary McCarthy co-starred Cherry Jones and Swoosie Kurtz. Producer Bill Haber and playwright Nora Ephron decided that they did not want photography of the actresses in character. In doing research, Julie Richards, my then assistant and a terrific designer herself, found this very sweet vintage photo of two girls in a hammock. It wasn't until I was actually presenting it that I realized how funny the image would be by adding the angry scrawls: "bitch" and "liar," as if the furious women each scribbled the words. I grabbed some magic markers and as soon as I defaced the photos, the room agreed in unison that we'd found our logo art. Nora Ephron sent me a lovely note the day our full page *New York Times* announcement appeared: "Thank you for an ad campaign that actually changed the play!"

Moguls & Movie Stars: A History of Hollywood (2010)

Very early in the process of producing his fantastic seven-part Turner Classic Movies (TCM) documentary, Bill Haber asked me to design a piece of art for use in a *Variety* ad he wanted to run announcing the project. My take on the subject matter was to picture the movie mogul as a modern day version of a Roman Emperor with his breastplate as a filmstrip and his cloak ornament a movie reel.

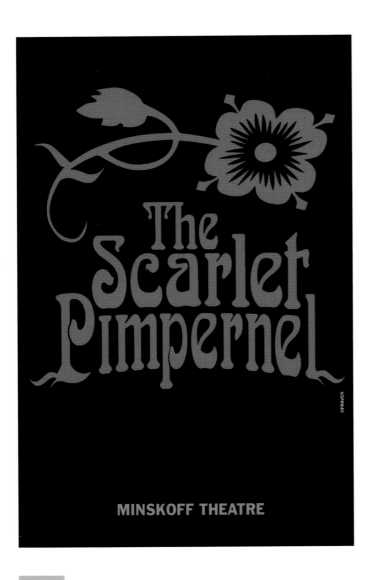

The Scarlet Pimpernel (1997

Some productions remain very special to me, and this is one of them. It marked the first time I worked with the fantastic producer Bill Haber. Although this musical wound up having two completely different poster variations during its run, this logo remained constant. The pimpernel flower had a very distinctive shape that lent itself well to graphic interpretation. The premiere production was lavish and spectacular, as well as a hell of a lot of fun to work on.

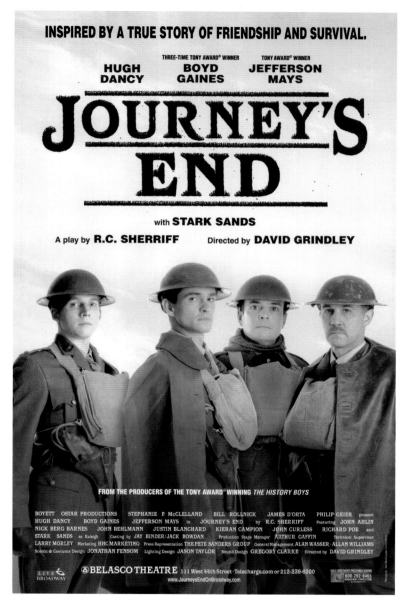

Photography by Jean-Marie Guyaux

Producer Bill Haber took a big chance bringing this show to Broadway. It was a gamble that paid off; the production received some of the best reviews I've ever read for a play, and won numerous honors, including the Tony Award for Best Play Revival. I was asked to recreate the look they had established for the London production. Photographer Jean-Marie Guyaux was meticulous and lit it beautifully. You'd never know that no more than two of the actors were in the studio at the same time. The immense talents of Hugh Dancy, Boyd Gaines, Jefferson Mays, and Stark Sands made these shoots very pleasant experiences.

Electra (1998)

There already existed this great photograph of star Zoë Wanamaker shot by T Charles Erickson from the Donmar Warehouse production. I experimented on it with various techniques, but much preferred the outcome of overexposing it and burning out most of the details. Producers Anita Waxman and Eric Krebs requested a contemporary look for the title treatment. I took my design in a corporate direction, which I feel was a great contrast to the classic image. The logo read from many blocks away when shining over Broadway from its Barrymore Theatre marquee. Needless to say, the production was amazing!

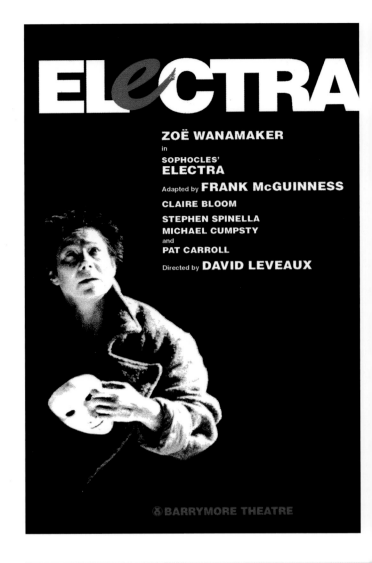

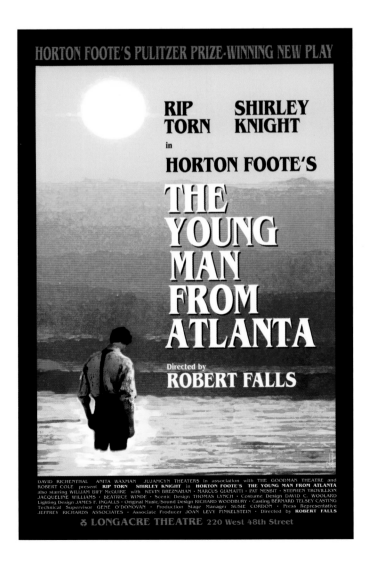

The Young Man from Atlanta (1997)

The artwork for this particular show stands out in my mind for one reason: I was experimenting with finally abandoning my drawing board for a computer. Using Photoshop for the first time was daunting, but after countless days of trial and error, I was very pleased with the results. What I didn't realize was (due to my inexperience with my new Mac), the illustration I created was only one inch high! Starting it from scratch again was infuriating but I certainly learned a lot about Photoshop.

Burn This (1987)

This graphic was very bold and versatile. It was one of the numerous logos I created over the years using a trusty copy machine, which is great for breaking type down and giving it an unusual rough edge. It made for a striking poster and marquee. The animation created for our fifteen-second television spots, in which the rubber stamp provocatively catches fire, was very effective. The show opened to critical acclaim and became a huge success due in no small part to John Malkovich's unforgettable performance!

Photography by Joan Marcus

Taller Than a Dwarf (2000)

Sometimes the teenage movie fan inside me cannot contain himself. As a lover of the suspense/horror genre, I was obsessing over the impending release of Wes Craven's *Scream 3*. There I was, at Joan Marcus's photography studio, anxiously awaiting the arrival of our stars, Matthew Broderick and Parker Posey. I knew that Ms. Posey had just finished filming *Scream 3* and I was determined to find out about her part in it. As you can see from the poster, the actors were asked to lean as far back as possible in order to ward off the looming title design. The final art, of course, I manipulated in Photoshop. Mr. Broderick said the pose gave him flashbacks to his recent *Godzilla* movie, where he spent much of the time looking up and leaning backwards. But, try as I might, I couldn't get Parker Posey to reveal any *Scream 3* secrets!

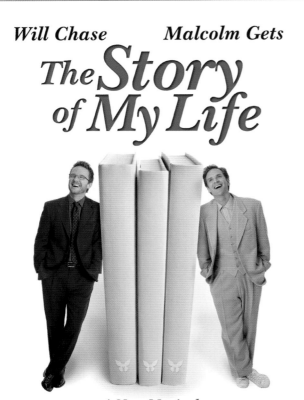

The Story of My Life (2009)

As always, it's a pleasure working with Richard Maltby Jr., this time as director. The show has a beautiful score by Neil Bartram and wonderful book by Brian Hill, which helped to make this an experience to treasure. My friend Carole Haber joining Chase Mishkin as producer was icing on the cake! Once my concept of using the actors as bookends was approved, I hired photographer Jean-Marie Guyaux to shoot it. Everything was kept on a stark white background, which reflected the look of the luscious set design by Robert Brill. Working on this musical will always hold a special place for me.

Photography by Jean-Marie Guyaux

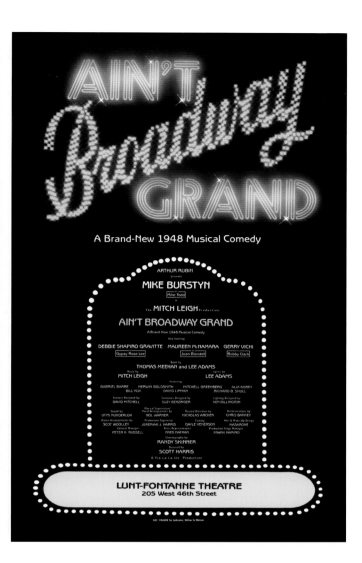

A Brand-New 1948 Musical Comedy

ARTHUR RUBIN
presents
MIKE BURSTYN
Mike Todd

The MITCH LEIGH Production
of
AIN'T BROADWAY GRAND
A Brand-New 1948 Musical Comedy
Also Starring
DEBBIE SHAPIRO GRAVITTE   MAUREEN McNAMARA   GERRY VICHI
Gypsy Rose Lee   Joan Blondell   Bobby Clark

Book by
THOMAS MEEHAN and LEE ADAMS
Music by   Lyrics by
MITCH LEIGH   LEE ADAMS
Featuring
GABRIEL BARRE   MERWIN GOLDSMITH   MITCHELL GREENBERG   ALIX KOREY
BILL KUX   DAVID LIPMAN   RICHARD B. SHULL
Scenery Designed by   Costumes Designed by   Lighting Designed by
DAVID MITCHELL   SUZY BENZINGER   KEN BILLINGTON

Sound by   Musical Supervision/   Musical Direction by   Orchestrations by
OTTS MUNDERLOH   Vocal Arrangements by   NICHOLAS ARCHER   CHRIS BANKEY
                  NEIL WARNER
Dance Arrangements by   Production Supervisor   Casting   Hair & Make-up Design
SCOT WOOLLEY   JEREMIAH J. HARRIS   GAYLE HENDERSON   NASARONE
General Manager   Press Representative   Production Stage Manager
PETER H. RUSSELL   FRED NATHAN   FRANK MARINO
Choreography by
RANDY SKINNER
Directed by
SCOTT HARRIS
A Tra La La Inc. Production

LUNT-FONTANNE THEATRE
205 West 46th Street

ART: FRAVER for LaDonna, Wilber & Warner

I cannot say I remember much about the show, but going to meetings at Mitch Leigh's office with my boss was always something of an event. Leigh was typically dressed in a black velour running suit sporting a rather large cigar that I honestly never recall him lighting. As you faced his desk, there he sat with a spectacular vista of Broadway behind him, this being the upper floor of a theatre district office building. I was never more entertained by bluster as he related various theatre stories. Everything he said sounded important. Mr. Leigh's manner led one to believe that there were follow-spots trailing his every move. He was a true Damon Runyon character, updated, and brought to life!

It Ain't Nothin' But the Blues (1999)

Quite honestly, the reason I was so excited to be designing the artwork for this production was because it was to be mounted at the Vivian Beaumont Theater at Lincoln Center. Instead of a traditional marquee, the Beaumont reproduces the show title designs in neon and houses them very prominently in their massive entrance windows. The show was a surprise hit and even lasted long enough to move out of Lincoln Center (bye, bye, neon!) and into the Ambassador Theatre on Broadway.

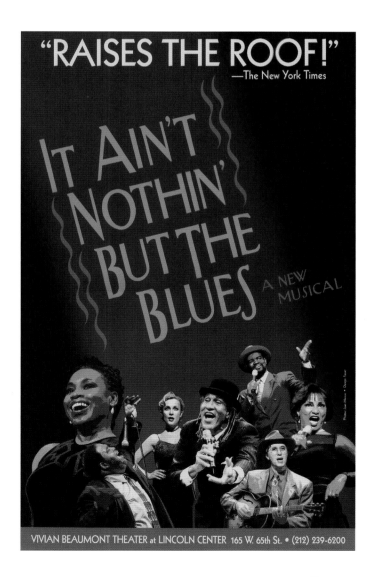

"RAISES THE ROOF!"
—The New York Times

IT AIN'T NOTHIN' BUT THE BLUES
A NEW MUSICAL

VIVIAN BEAUMONT THEATER at LINCOLN CENTER 165 W. 65th St. • (212) 239-6200

Photography by Joan Marcus

I have always loved theatre posters. The art of a good theatre poster is not only beautiful, but evocative in a particular way that draws me into the world of the play it's representing.

I have known Frank since we were relative babies. I had assumed the role of the platinum blonde, Lily Garland, in *On the Twentieth Century* and he was the art director for the show. He kindly agreed to create a poster for me when I played the iconic New York cabaret Reno Sweeney's. The act was an opportunity to introduce my brunette self to New York. So, Frank created a wonderful poster, a portrait sans hair. It left the act to answer the question, "What does she actually look like?" I have that drawing in an honored place in my home. And, forty years later, it reminds me of his gorgeous and clever artistry every time I look at it. Thanks, Frank!

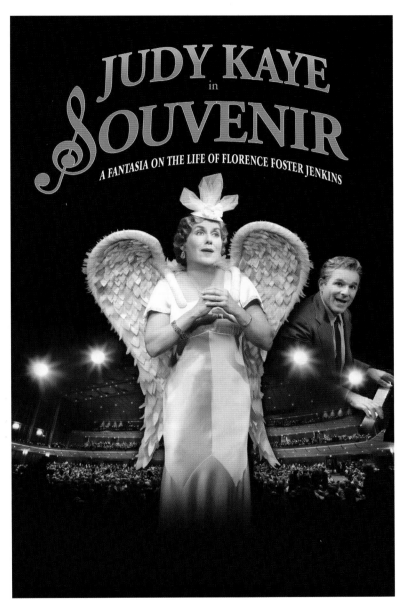

Photography by Carol Rosegg

The glorious Judy Kaye took on the role of Florence Foster Jenkins, an American socialite and amateur soprano who, due to her technical incompetence, became somewhat of a sensation in New York City during the early part of the twentieth century. Part of my function in the agency, aside from designing theatre poster art, was to act as creative director for radio advertising. To record this sixty-second spot, I worked with the fantastic writer and producer Tex Hauser. It featured a grand announcer build up that led to Judy Kaye, as Florence, singing an aria totally off-key. The commercial was hilarious, and was approved by everyone involved. When it hit the radio, the agency was flooded with phone calls, mainly from doctors' offices, complaining that our star's atonal singing was disturbing their waiting room patients. The agency had booked a lot of airtime, which was quickly funneled into other media, when the spot was whisked off the radio.

A Doll's Life (1982)

Director Harold Prince placed an urgent call to the advertising agency asking to send me out to Los Angeles as soon as possible. He wanted me to create new art for his musical, which was about to premiere at the Ahmanson Theatre. No one was happy with the existing artwork. After sitting through a preview performance, I was told by press agent Mary Bryant, that Mr. Prince expected me to have art to present to him within a couple of days. Normally I have at least two weeks to come up with concepts and present art! No pressure, right? It was clear from seeing the show that the overall design was heavily influenced by painter Edvard Munch, famous for *The Scream*, (which was exactly what I felt like doing!). I created a total of twelve sketches done in the etching style used by the artist. When I told the press agent I was ready, I was assured that I was to present the work to Mr. Prince in a private setting, just the two of us. As I waited in a very small holding room in the bowels of the theatre, in walked Betty Comden and Adolph Green (the playwrights and lyricists). I introduced myself and they sat down as the "Larrys," Grossman (composer) and Fuller (choreographer) entered along with others. Well, before Mr. Prince even showed up, there were about nine people stuffed into this tiny room. Instead of dismissing the group, as I thought he would, Mr. Prince turned to me and said, "Okay, let's see them." I revealed the first drawing and before I could take a breath, I heard him say, "No. Next." I was hoping for a painless, instant death at that point. I presented the second drawing. "That's it! I love it!" He was clearly excited and the rest of the group responded in kind. Confident now, I said, "I have ten more." But Mr. Prince knows what he likes, "Put them away. That's the one." The room cleared out in about five seconds. I was in such a hurry to leave LA, I'd have flown the plane back myself. You can now see my work for *A Doll's Life* up close and on permanent exhibit at Joe Allen's Restaurant.

GEORGE HEARN   BETSY JOSLYN
in
A DOLL'S LIFE
A NEW MUSICAL

PETER GALLAGHER
EDMUND LYNDECK

Book and Lyrics by   Music by
BETTY   ADOLPH   LARRY
COMDEN and **GREEN   GROSSMAN**

Choreography by
LARRY FULLER

Production Directed by
HAROLD PRINCE

A NEW MUSICAL

MARK HELLINGER THEATER
51st Street West of Broadway

LIZ CALLAWAY
ACTRESS AND SINGER

They say, "You always remember your first time," and seeing your name on a Broadway poster for the first time is no different.

For me, it was the musical *Baby*, and what made it extra special was that the poster was created by designer Frank Verlizzo. Everyone in the theatre world was familiar with Frank's work under the name Fraver. His creations for *Sweeney Todd*, *Deathtrap*, and so many others were legendary. The idea that he was designing the poster for *Baby* was thrilling.

Frank's artwork for the theatre always zeroes in on a certain special element of the show. In this case it was the music. (*The New York Times* critic Frank Rich wrote that musicals like this "inspire you to run to the record store as soon as the original cast album comes out.") I'll never forget the first time I rounded 47th Street and saw the marquee of the Barrymore Theatre and those now iconic music notes beaming above me. And then they were on buses, on t-shirts, and on the cast album cover—which happened to be the first CD I owned! *Baby* had arrived, and the show had joined that rare collection of Fraver creations.

Early in my career I designed the logo for the highly successful Maltby-Shire musical revue *Starting Here, Starting Now.* I was very excited to be working again with Richard Maltby Jr. on this Broadway project. During the art presentation, producer Jim Freydberg was very much impressed with this bold logo graphic as opposed to the other art he had seen showing actual babies and baby paraphernalia. I used a trusty photostat machine to enlarge the music staff and notes. However, I did expose my complete lack of musical training. After the posters were printed, I met Richard Maltby on the street. He told me that he loved the poster I had designed but he asked why I had flopped and inverted some of the musical notes. "Because I cannot read music and they looked better that way," was my response. Fortunately, he has a sense of humor and is still speaking to me!

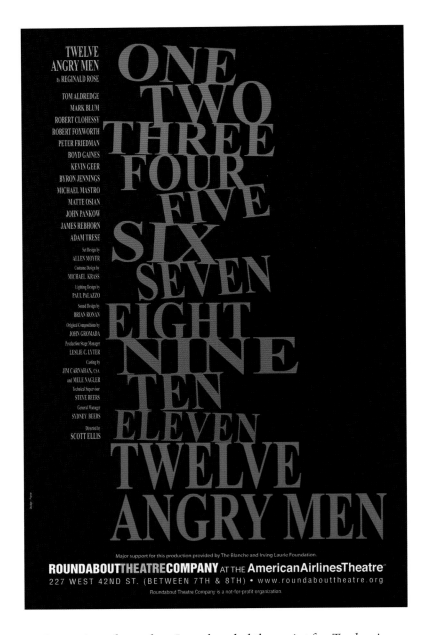

Strangely enough, I was serving on jury duty when I was handed the script for *Twelve Angry Men*. I had at my disposal the perfect setting for research. After designing a few comps, everything looked very generic to me. Gavels, courtrooms, jury boxes, marble facades, and the like just didn't look interesting. The characters in the play are given no names, just their assigned jury numbers: Juror One, Juror Two, etc. Ultimately, I decided to stay away from courtroom imagery and take my favorite route: graphic type design. Director Scott Ellis loved it so much, the folks at Roundabout Theatre felt compelled to use it. The show was a surprise hit, received rave reviews, and toured for two years!

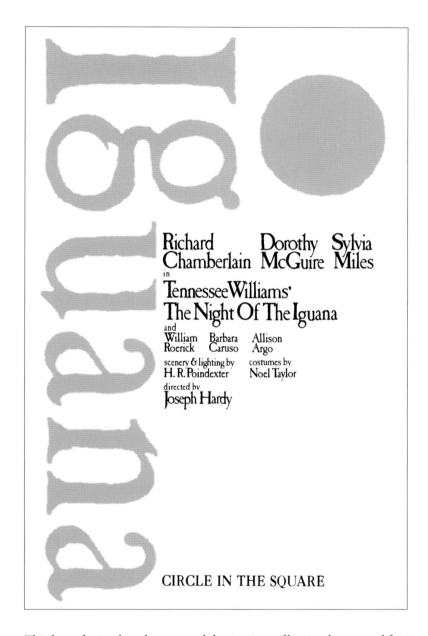

Richard   Dorothy   Sylvia
Chamberlain   McGuire   Miles
in
Tennessee Williams'
The Night Of The Iguana
and
William   Barbara   Allison
Roerick   Caruso   Argo
scenery & lighting by   costumes by
H. R. Poindexter   Noel Taylor
directed by
Joseph Hardy

CIRCLE IN THE SQUARE

This logo design has the unusual distinction of having been used for two different productions years apart but both produced by Circle in the Square Theatre. I designed it originally at Blaine Thompson for the version starring Richard Chamberlain. He gave a wonderful performance and even managed to not be overshadowed by the larger-than-life presence of Sylvia Miles at her blowsy best! Twelve years later, I was surprised to open *The New York Times* to see an ad announcing the second production—using my uncredited artwork! Since Circle in the Square produced both versions, they had the right to use the artwork again, but at the very least I felt they should restore my art credit in future ads. I wrote a letter with this request to ad man Jon Bierman of the Golden Group, Circle in the Square's ad agency. Fortunately, Circle in the Square agreed. Jon and I went on to become friends, working at two other ad agencies together, and every so often he shows me the letter for a laugh! *Iguana* is one of my favorite Tennessee Williams plays and I am very honored to have my artwork represent it twice on Broadway.

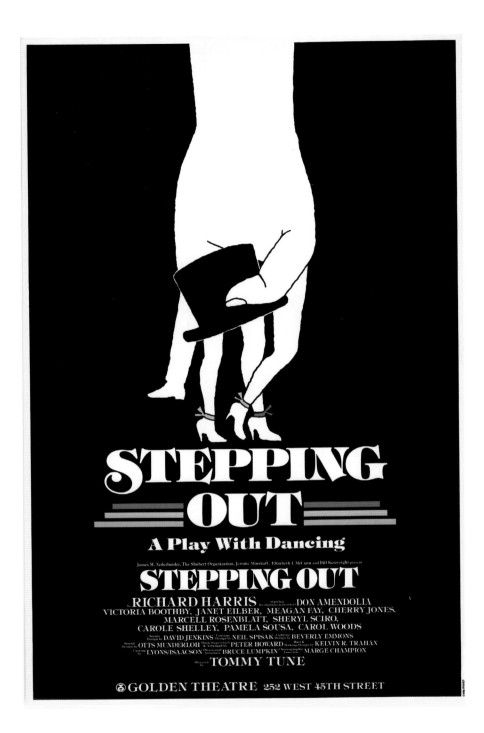

After winning multiple Tony Awards in various categories for *My One and Only*, and before working on *Grand Hotel*, Tommy Tune directed this fun play about a group of colorful folks who attend the same tap dancing class in a North London church hall. It was the first time I saw the sublime Cherry Jones on a Broadway stage. Tommy Tune reacted favorably to this poster. He said it meant something to him because he typically works out his choreography using his fingers.

Photography by Kenn Duncan. Courtesy of the New York Public Library for the Performing Arts

The word-of-mouth from its out-of-town tryout could not have been any worse. But it's amazing how with a new director, Tommy Tune, *My One and Only* turned out to be dazzling entertainment that earned nine Tony nominations and walked away with six awards! I based the poster art on the look of the show, which used very flat graphic shapes as set pieces. Kenn Duncan, renowned dance and theatre photographer, took the photo and I purchased the silver frame at Tiffany's to add an extra touch of class to an already-classy production.

Quilters (1984)

Admittedly, I do not recall much of the design process for this obscure production. I do like the haunting quality of my poster image. By far the most mysterious element of the entire event was how a show playing in a traditional Off-Broadway house managed to be nominated for six Tony Awards, including Best Musical, after a run of only twenty-four performances.

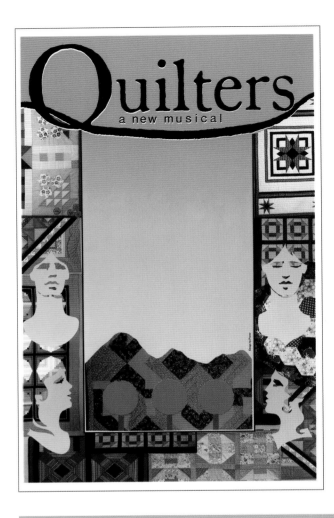

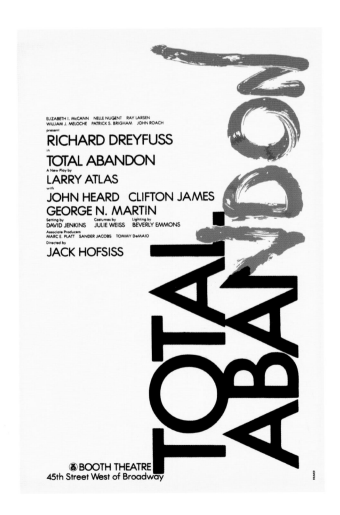

Total Abandon (1983)

Richard Dreyfuss on Broadway! It is not very often that a movie star of such high caliber came to Broadway in a new play about child abuse! The staff at Serino, Coyne & Nappi were preparing an enormous art presentation for the hottest producing team at the time, Liz McCann and Nelle Nugent. Our offices were very informal and I remember Liz walking in one day to look over my shoulder as I was finger painting, creating this graphic. The next week, the presentation occurred, some choices were made, and changes requested. My artwork fell by the wayside as things moved in a different direction. The revision process went on for numerous rounds with no end in sight. Nobody seemed happy with anything. Both staff and freelance artists were frantically trying to come up with a solution. The day of the deadline for finished art approached—the conference room was crowded with all the revised artwork that had been created over the past weeks. I remember things seeming very grim as the producers looked everything over yet again. Then, Liz turned to me and said, "Remember that finger painting art? I like that. Let's use it." Generally, I believe that if the producers are having a great deal of difficulty deciding on the artwork, then the production is probably going through the same ordeal. *Total Abandon* had seven previews and closed on opening night.

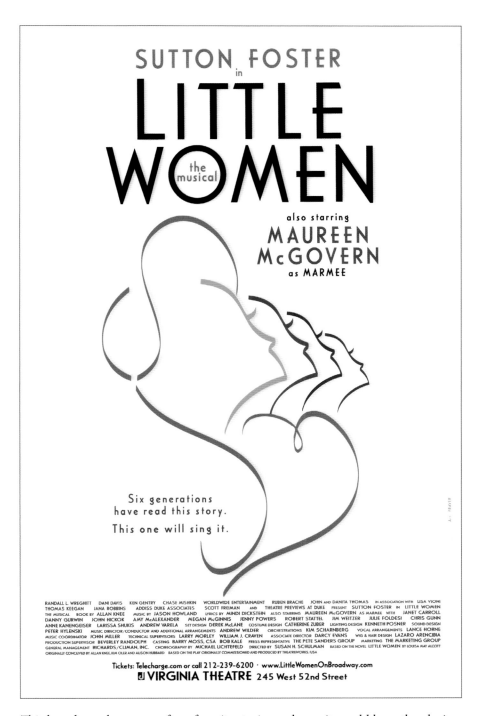

This has always been one of my favorite stories and now it would have the glorious music of Jason Howland. The show starred the immensely talented Sutton Foster and the dreamy Danny Gurwin. I first worked on the show while at Grey Entertainment where I'd art directed a version of the poster created by Raphal Oblinski, a master illustrator. The production was then delayed, during which time, I'd moved to Rave! Advertising. When production resumed, the producers now felt the lyrical Oblinski art was too traditional looking. This is where I created the linear graphic "ribbon" girls for the new poster art. So the project I began at Grey and continued at Rave!, was finally finished at the Eliran Murphy Group. The art is a modern take on the typical *Little Women* image: Marmee's four daughters.

Bill KENWRIGHT
presents

Jessica
LANGE

Tennessee WILLIAMS'
The GLASS
MENAGERIE

with
Dallas   Sarah
ROBERTS   PAULSON
and
Josh
LUCAS

Directed by
David
LEVEAUX

BARRYMORE THEATRE 243 West 47th Street

Design: Fraver • Photography: Gasper Tringale

Photography by Gasper Tringale

The Glass Menagerie (2005)

There had already been a wonderful shoot with the great photographer Gasper Tringale and star Jessica Lange. But my biggest thrill came when I had to arrange to meet Ms. Lange for her photo approval. She was Christmas shopping and needed a break, so she chose a diner on lower Fifth Avenue to meet for coffee while discussing the images. Nothing beats waiting outside of a restaurant in NYC watching a luminous movie star walking down the street knowing she's heading toward YOU. What a rush!

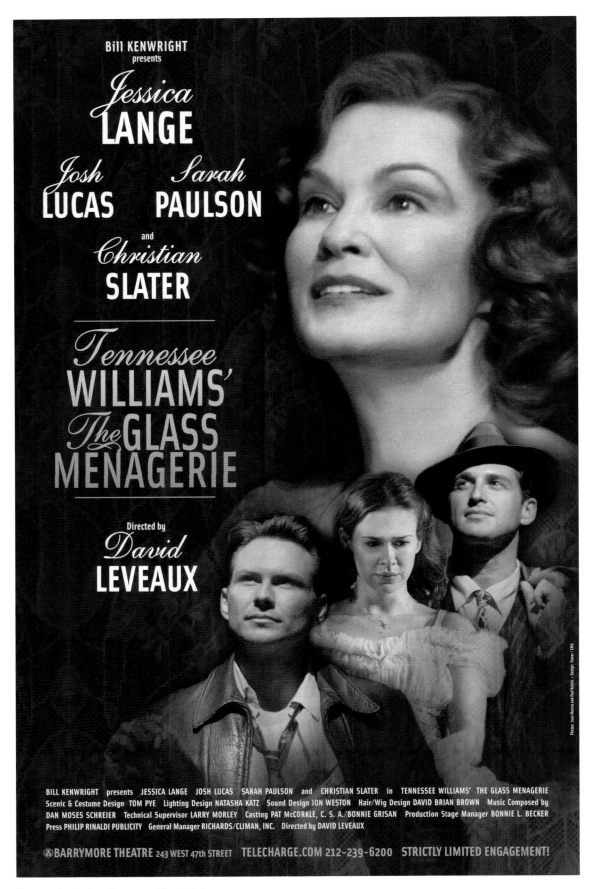

Photography by Joan Marcus and Paul Kolnik

This 2005 revival of Tennessee Williams's classic *The Glass Menagerie* gave Frank and me the opportunity to work once again with the great British producer Bill Kenwright. Bill announced the production, starring the magnificent Jessica Lange, as a limited twenty-week engagement.

As always, Frank designed an elegant logo and poster that featured a stunning and dramatic portrait photo of Ms. Lange, shot by Gasper Tringale. Then, as occasionally happens during pre-production, the actor playing Tom changed prior to opening—and unfortunately, we had already printed the poster with his name on it! So once the role was recast, we used production photography (this time shot by Joan Marcus and Paul Kolnik), with Jessica and the other three supporting actors.

Frank designed the second poster showcasing the actors in costume, layered on a textured brown background that mirrored the set, all while retaining Frank's original logo design. The show opened and received mixed reviews, and while we had strong initial advance sales, the advance slowly began to diminish thereafter.

It is at this point a production often changes the look of its advertising. Bill asked Frank to design a third look, and as usual, Frank came through with another beautiful poster. This one featured a montage of the actors against a lighter, cream-colored background while once again retaining the original logotype. In retrospect, all three pieces of art showcase Frank's extraordinary and versatile talent as a designer.

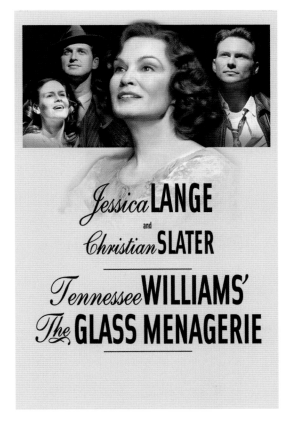

Photography by Joan Marcus and Paul Kolnik

It was an absolute thrill to be working on my second David Merrick production. The first had been Tom Stoppard's Tony Award-winning play, *Travesties*, but I was just starting out in the art department and wasn't a part of the ad meetings. Now, I was presenting the art and was going to meet him. Unfortunately, Mr. Merrick had suffered a stroke a few years earlier and was somewhat reliant on a wheelchair. What no one had mentioned was that he couldn't speak. It was mighty weird having David Merrick's assistant "translate" his series of grunts and arm gestures as valid criticism, but we managed. And, naturally, the poster was printed in his official color, Merrick Red. Four years later, I was art directing the advertising for his musical revival *Oh, Kay!* He seemed in better health and spirits. I presented the double-truck quote ad layout to him one morning at the Richard Rodgers Theatre, while he was seated in the aisle on an elaborately bejeweled prop throne. Ever the showman!

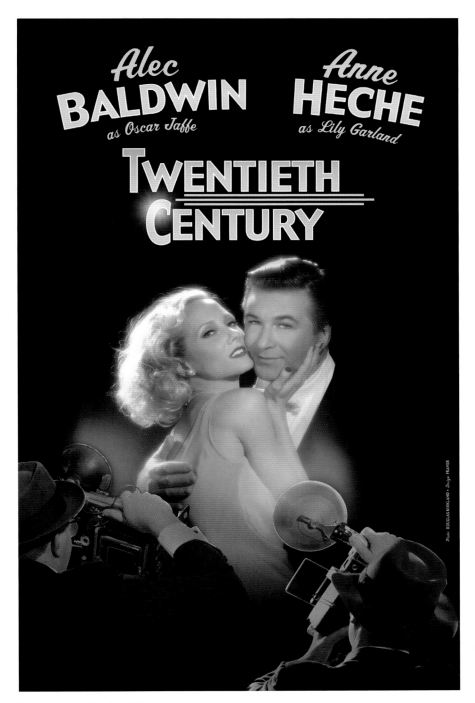

Photography by Douglas Kirkland

Based on the design I put together using vintage movie posters, director Walter Bobbie asked Roundabout Theatre Company to fly us out to Los Angeles to shoot Alec Baldwin and Anne Heche for the poster art. I hired the legendary photographer Douglas Kirkland (who is famous for his Marilyn Monroe sessions) to make my art come to life. It was definitely exciting and certainly not the norm to be at the Kirkland studio in the Hollywood Hills shooting two big stars as if it were 1932!

Actor Vincent Price had always been a favorite of mine from movies like *Laura, House on Haunted Hill,* and *Theatre of Blood.* I drew his portrait as Oscar Wilde and then I turned to the trusty office copier to create this Victorian effect of antique printing. Mr. Price was a riveting actor, as marvelous on stage as he was on film. It was an honor for me to design this Broadway poster.

Show art is often created before it is cast or begins rehearsal. The art must create the right expectations for the show, which is also the primary responsibility of the press agent. For *The Merchant*, Frank found a public domain etching at the New York Public Library and "aged" it to look like it came from medieval times.

The Merchant was Arnold Wesker's version of Shakespeare's story told from the Jewish point of view. With his image of a stern old Jew, Frank showed us who was the focus of the play and who we should root for. While the image did not remotely resemble Zero Mostel, who played Shylock (briefly), it somehow conveyed his spirit.

Show art must be adaptable as well as catch your attention and draw you to the play. It can't give away too much but just enough to intrigue. Not only does it need to somehow accommodate billing and theatre information, it must also "read" from a huge billboard in Times Square as well as in a tiny listing online or a one column ad in the *New York Times*.

While it is difficult to know exactly what makes someone purchase a ticket for a particular show, surveys show that the visual image and how it affects you, even subliminally, can be the deciding factor.

Do
you
want
to
know
a secret?

LARRY
BRYGGMAN

MICHAEL
HAYDEN

ALI
MACGRAW

JULIANNA
MARGULIES

JEREMY
SISTO

FESTEN

MUSIC BOX THEATRE
239 West 45th Street

Photography by Joan Marcus

Producer Bill Kenwright brought the London smash hit *Festen* to Broadway with a phenomenal US cast. I met with famous theatre photographer Joan Marcus a few hours before our scheduled photo session. She was assigned to shoot the portraits that I would use to create the poster art, as well as the photos the press agent would send to the media. The actors were getting their hair and make-up done and started filing in when they were ready for the camera. I must admit, the movie-star-struck teenager in me took over when Ali MacGraw entered. I had always read that she was amazingly beautiful, but the description doesn't do her any justice. And that Hollywood aura! I just remember trying to remain cool as I leaned over to Joan and said under my breath, "Ali MacGraw, Joan! ALI MACGRAW!" She leaned over to me and whispered, "I feel like I'm twelve again." I'm sure we were both motionless for a few minutes, staring, when Ms. MacGraw spoke up pleasantly, "I'm ready when you are."

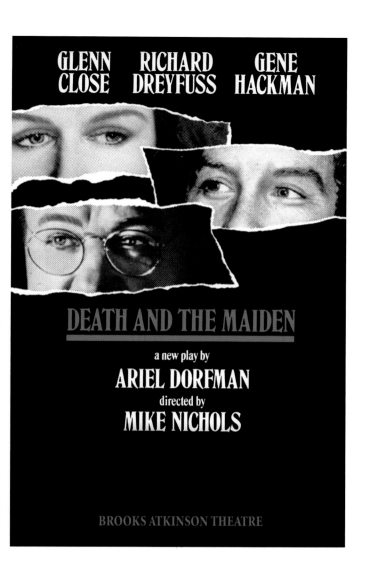

Death and the Maiden (1992)

Before designing this poster, I asked director Mike Nichols for images of his above-title superstars. He secured the rights for these three. To begin, I screened the portraits to obtain the dotted-texture authenticity of an old newsprint reproduction, as if torn from headlines of the day. The play is a tightly wound suspense melodrama set in a time when an unnamed South American country had just overthrown its dictator for a budding democratic government. Tearing photos has always been a favorite device of mine ever since Gil Lesser taught me the art of manipulation. In fact, this poster incorporates all of my favorite design elements: color scheme, intense eyes, and ripped paper. It was a glittery, star-studded opening night, noteworthy to me because I sat across the aisle from John F. Kennedy Jr!

Fortune's Fool (2002)

Producer Julian Schlossberg was very excited to be venturing from Off-Broadway to Broadway with this star vehicle. I had two fantastic faces to work with and a plethora of photography to work from. My biggest challenge came from an unexpected source. When I presented the various pieces of art to the producing team, they all seemed concerned about one thing: the thinning hairlines of their stars. The actors weren't going to be wearing wigs. Retouching can only do so much. I thought my solution rather ingenious: to crop the photo severely at the top and place the title treatment on it. It looks deliberate, strong, and graphic. Both Alan Bates and Frank Langella won acting Tony Awards for this wonderful show—and no one ever missed seeing the tops of their heads!

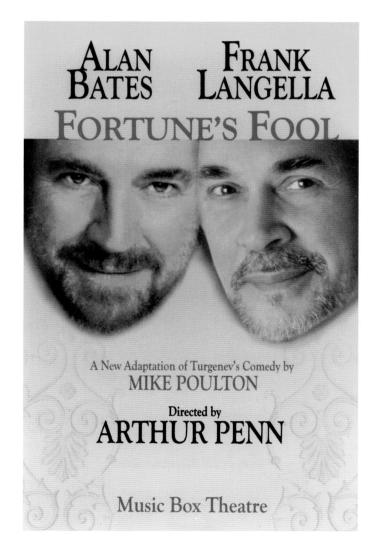

Television legend Valerie Harper portrays Tallulah Bankhead during a period of time when she'd just finished what was to be her last movie, the dreadful horror film *Die! Die! My Darling*! Based on an actual event, the play, by the fabulous Matthew Lombardo, is an uproarious tribute to an actress whose tabloid exploits almost superseded her theatrical triumphs. I have been collecting vintage movie posters since my days at the High School of Art and Design. There is a certain amount of controlled chaos that I imagine went into designing most of them. Studio bosses and industry distributors had much to say in terms of marketing their film product. It was very exciting for me to recreate the look of a 1965 movie poster for *Looped*. I used Walter McBride's phenomenal photograph of Ms. Harper as the centerpiece of my montage. Over the years, I have been a great fan of both Valerie Harper and Tallulah Bankhead (*Lifeboat*—by Hitchcock—Amazing!) so getting to work on this project made me absolutely ecstatic.

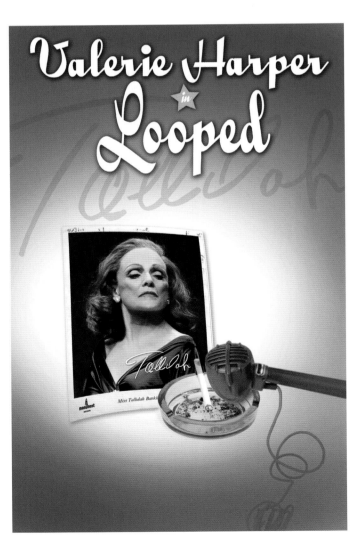

Photography by Carol Rosegg

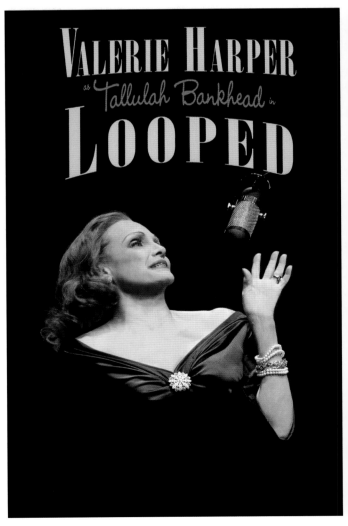

Photography by Carol Rosegg

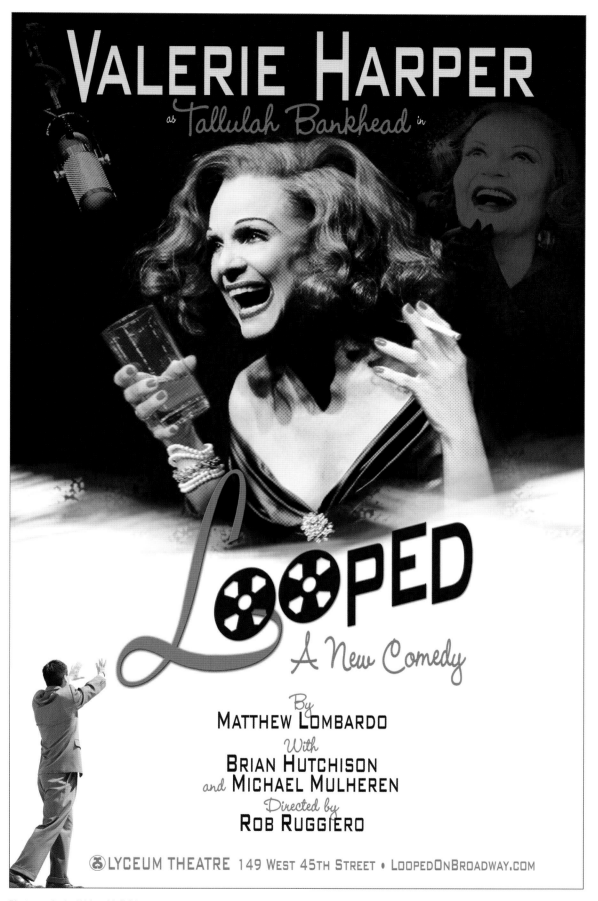

VALERIE HARPER

as Tallulah Bankhead *in*

LOOPED

A New Comedy

By
MATTHEW LOMBARDO
With
BRIAN HUTCHISON
and MICHAEL MULHEREN
Directed by
ROB RUGGIERO

LYCEUM THEATRE 149 WEST 45TH STREET • LOOPEDONBROADWAY.COM

Photography by Walter McBride

This poster couldn't be simpler, yet it proved very effective. Since David Copperfield couldn't be in NYC in time for a shoot, I drew his eyes, screened the drawing, and then ghosted the entire image. I remember meeting him at a TGI Fridays restaurant (of all places!) on Times Square, where he showed up with his famous-model girlfriend and proceeded to explain how he wanted me to design a billboard overlooking the TKTS booth that would perform some sort of magic/ESP every half hour. The idea sounded terrific. Needless to say, for budgetary reasons it never went much further than our hamburger lunch!

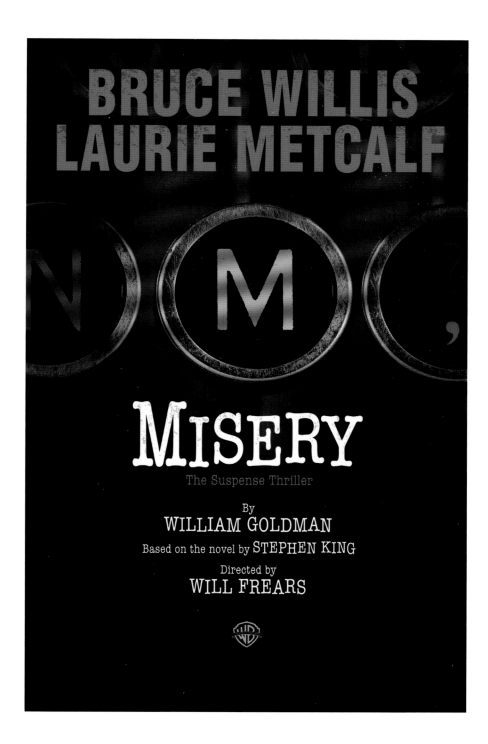

I was thrilled to be asked by Mark Kaufman and Raymond Wu from Warner Bros. to design the poster art for their stage adaptation of Stephen King's *Misery*. Here is a really scary story that, although simple on its surface, is filled with hundreds of images worth exploring graphically. In my years of advertising, if I've learned nothing else, it is that simple is better. Simple allows you to stand out from all the visual clutter. Creating an easily memorable icon is also imperative. The producers were immediately attracted to this concept of the vintage typewriter key.

THE AMERICAN THEATRE WING'S

TONY AWARDS 2001®

THE LEAGUE OF AMERICAN THEATRES
AND PRODUCERS AND
THE AMERICAN THEATRE WING
PRESENT THE 55TH ANNUAL
ANTOINETTE PERRY AWARDS
SUNDAY, JUNE 3, 2001

The Tony Awards (1996, 2001, 2003)

There is a wealth of stage pictures and concepts an artist can conjure to design a poster representing Broadway's highest honor! Having the image of the actual award appear on the artwork in some way, shape, or form was the single directive. That being said, the requirement was waived in 1996 for the 50th Annual Antoinette Perry Awards program cover and posters, although I cannot remember the reason. It was always a fun challenge to be given the freedom to basically do whatever I wanted for the poster, which, honestly, is not as easy as it sounds. Naturally, there was still the client approval process. The three posters I designed were vastly different, my favorite being the 2001 poster. It is a fairly straightforward treatment with the focus being on the words rather than the prize itself. Adding those Mondrian-like shapes with dashes of color was a playful way of livening up the stately design.

The Lion King (1997)

Among the most famous theatre posters worldwide is the image for Disney's groundbreaking musical, *The Lion King*. I led the design of it for Disney Theatrical Productions in 1997 when I was at Grey Entertainment. Unlike many shows for which I had previously developed artwork, *The Lion King* was already a successful animated film, so this project introduced a challenging opportunity to create something new and fresh for a title that came with existing perceptions.

For inspiration, I recalled the cave painting image of Simba from having seen the film in the early 1990s. Julie Taymor's costume sketches and Richard Hudson's scenic designs served as references for the look of the Broadway show, which was heavily stylized with African influences. The graphic nature of the board patterns on Ms. Taymor's costumes specifically had a huge influence on my approach to the show art.

The lion's mane presented a challenge. There were so many ways to treat and interpret it. I eventually drew by hand at least 50 other Simba head sketches until I was seeing them in my sleep. My original version of the head was somewhat rounded in shape, but then producer Thomas Schumacher enlisted legendary Disney animator Hans Bacher to distill my initial design into what became the woodcut-like icon still used to advertise the show over 20 years later.

Its simplicity and use of solid black, red, and yellow made *The Lion King* poster distinctive. Mr. Schumacher, his co-producer Peter Schneider, and Ms. Taymor were immediately drawn to it. As a result, the bold-type design (based on a Neuland font) never changed and the bright taxi cab-yellow background remained as I'd first presented it.

CHAPTER TWO
SONDHEIM

SUNDAY in the PARK with GEORGE

A Musical

The Shubert Organization and Emanuel Azenberg
by arrangement with
Playwrights Horizons
present

Mandy   Bernadette
Patinkin   Peters
in

SUNDAY in the PARK
with GEORGE
A Musical

Music and Lyrics by
Stephen Sondheim

Book by
James Lapine

Scenery by   Costumes by   Lighting by
Tony   Patricia   Ann   Richard
Straiges Zipprodt and Hould-Ward   Nelson

Special Effects by   Sound by   Hair and Makeup
Bran Ferren   Tom Morse   Lo Presto/Allen

Musical Direction by   Orchestrations by   Movement by
Paul   Michael   Randolyn
Gemignani   Starobin   Zinn

Directed by
James Lapine

Ⓢ Booth Theatre 45th Street West of Broadway

Photography by John Reilly

BERNADETTE PETERS
ACTRESS, SINGER, AND CHILDREN'S BOOK AUTHOR

When you're doing a show, I think everyone's energy in the theatre goes into making a success. From the ushers to the box office, everyone's drive goes toward what's happening on the stage and points to it. Frank's poster art for *Sunday in the Park with George* and *Follies* is included in that energy as well. I thank Steve Sondheim all the time for giving me things to sing about—real things, interesting, and important things. I never really sing a song just because it's pretty. It must give me something genuine to talk about or sing about! Frank gives us the story and the musicality in the form of a graphic image. I was amazed when I first saw the poster for *Sunday in the Park with George* because Frank had captured the difference between the first and second acts. It was very inventive of him. I know as an artist, he must find the same inspiration in creating the poster designs for a Sondheim musical as I do in singing his songs. From first viewing of Frank's *Follies* poster at the Kennedy Center, one can tell instantly that it is a story about heartache, and the ghosts these people carry around with them.

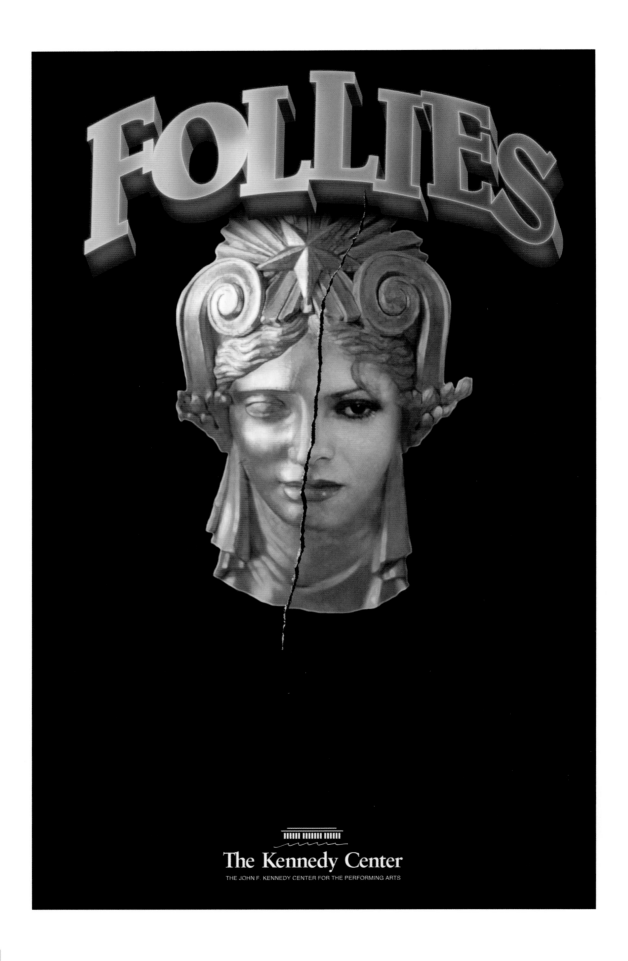

Follies (2011)

I created twelve different posters for my *Follies* art presentation. Each one focused on a different aspect of the musical. These are a sampling of the range of concepts.

Roger Berlind
presents

**John Rubinstein   Terrence Mann
Christine Ebersole**

Getting Away With Murder

by
Stephen Sondheim and **George Furth**

with
**Kandis Chappell   Frankie Faison
Jodi Long   Josh Mostel**

and

**Al Espinosa   Herb Foster
Michelle Hurd   William Ragsdale**

Scenic Design	Lighting Design	Costume Design
Douglas W. Schmidt	Kenneth Posner	Robert Wojewodski

Sound Design	Special Effects Design	Fight Director	Casting
Jeff Ladman	Gregory Meeh	Steve Rankin	Jay Binder

General Manager	Press Representative	Production Stage Manager
Marvin A. Krauss	Bill Evans & Assoc.	Jeff Lee

Directed by
Jack O'Brien

World Premiere at The Old Globe Theatre, San Diego, California
Artistic Director, Jack O'Brien • Managing Director, Thomas Hall

Getting Away With Murder

A Comedy Thriller

🜨 **Broadhurst Theatre** 44th Street West of Broadway

Getting Away with Murder (1996)

It was an incredible amount of fun working on this show with producer Roger Berlind. I love murder mysteries and of course, anytime I can get to meet with Stephen Sondheim is a cause for celebration in my book. Both men fell immediately in love with my image of the revolver-toting gargoyle. I found him at a Pennsylvania flea market and thought he would be perfect. The poster was used as presented, with no changes whatsoever (a rarity!). Unfortunately, the show was pelted with negative reviews. Giving credit due to gentleman producer Roger Berlind, he approved running the *New York Times*'s "last 12 performances" ad with the image of our devilish icon now holding the gun to his own head with a quote from noted critic Linda Winer, "The gargoyle is adorable!"

For this poster, I thought I'd create a very funny, though sophisticated, image. When it was presented, the wonderful Bernard Gersten, executive producer of Lincoln Center Theater, didn't like it at all and said it was "too silly-looking" to represent one of their shows. After a few months and many pieces of art later, however, my martini-guzzling amphibian persevered. I suspect that the play's adapter Nathan Lane and director Susan Stroman eventually felt the image captured the feeling of their musical better than was supposed months earlier!

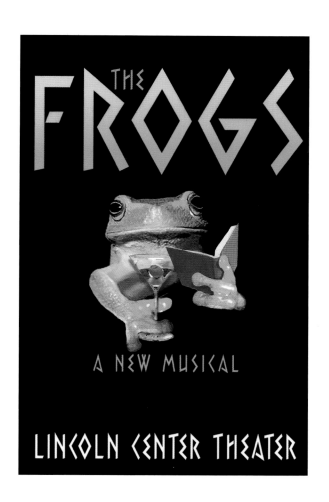

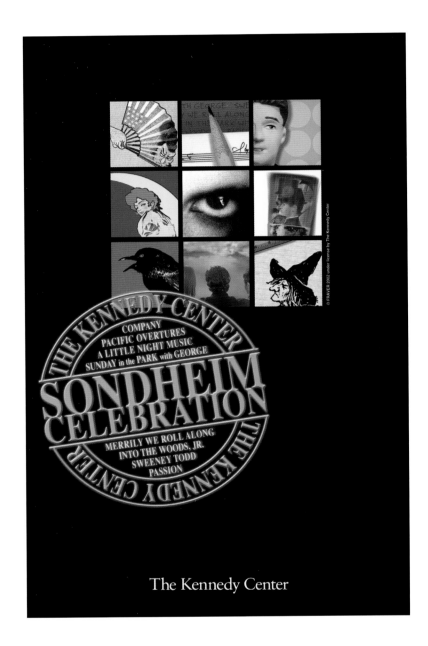

Max Woodward and David Kitto from the Kennedy Center contacted me about this massive project. It was a major career highlight to be invited to create artwork for this highly anticipated event. Originally, I was asked to design one poster to represent the entire Celebration. As usual, I approached the project a number of ways. When I came up with this concept featuring fragments of art from the various productions, I made much more work for myself. Obviously, I would need to design nine individual posters in order to extract a detail from each one. I wanted to convey the individuality of each production but the holism of the celebration itself. I started with an underlying graphic device: a circle. It appears in different ways in each poster. It is the graphic foundation, the starting point, and a way of tying things together. Kennedy Center president, Michael Kaiser, and his staff couldn't have been more enthusiastic about the presentation. This was a joyous project from start to finish, and the productions were brilliant.

COMMENTARY

JARED BRADSHAW
ACTOR AND SINGER

What's a Fraver?

FRAnk VERlizzo. The first time I saw FRAVER on a poster was in ALL CAPS but hidden in the demon barber's shadow under a rather maniacal cartoon of Sweeney Todd, and, well, Angela Lansbury. At least I think that was her. She was scarier, and was tugging on Sweeney's tailcoat . . . was she pulling him back or asking him, "Please, Mr. Todd, may I play too?"

This has always been my favorite showcard/poster art. It sure didn't seem like 1979 (the year I was born . . . that was disco) it seemed like it was from 200 years ago, black and white, and the only color was blood red . . . on his hands, the razor, her apron. In very creepy letters. Was this a font? This illustration told us all we needed to know about the plot going in. Get ready for a show you've never experienced before.

I collect Broadway showcards, I have 400 or so. I started collecting in college. I covered my walls with them. It was as close as a boy from Georgia could get to New York. It made me feel like a part of things. The more I knew, the better my chances of making it. The first set I collected were Sondheim's shows: *Sweeney Todd, Merrily We Roll Along, Pacific Overtures, A Little Night Music, Sunday in the Park with George, Company, Getting Away with Murder, The Frogs, Follies*, it goes on and on. I wanted cowboy boots because the 1980's George was wearing them in the bottom half of the *Sunday* poster FRAVER designed. Another time he perfectly told the plot of the show in one image. A couple in a painting, and then the same couple seemingly today . . . 100 years later. How does one come up with these things? A gargoyle with a gun . . . a philosophical frog with a book and a martini . . .

In the summer of 2002, I was right out of college doing summer stock in Charlotte, North Carolina, and Charlottesville, Virginia, and every couple of weeks, I drove up to Washington, DC, to see the Sondheim Celebration! Imagine . . . an entire summer of seven Sondheim shows IN REP! I saw them all. And, "Joy to the world Sweeney Todd is here!" (just like the quote poster I had at home, on one of my four Sweeney Todd posters) in the gift shop was a festival of its own: tons of merchandise, mugs, shirts, hats, notepads, mousepads, scarves, pillows, and a brand new *Sweeney Todd* poster! A new *Sunday* poster . . . a new *Night Music* poster . . . and FRAVER did them! That guy? The guy whose name is on the bottom of all the posters I have at home . . . I do research . . . he designed my *Scarlet Pimpernel, The Lion King*?! It goes on and on. I have to meet this man. (I bought the whole collectible FRAVER portfolio poster set. How could I NOT? This was made for me.)

Lucky me! Fast forward four more years. I book a dream show Off-Broadway . . . the long running *Forbidden Broadway*, where I get to play Bobby in *Company* and *Sweeney Todd* and Stephen Sondheim himself in our *Sunday in the Park with George* skit! And I got to invite Michael Cerveris and Raúl Esparza and Stephen Sondheim to come see me play them. A gift indeed. But best of all, FRAVER was designing the posters! I was part of a show that FRAVER was working on. I wasn't in summer stock any more.

That edition was *Forbidden Broadway: Special Victims Unit*, and I got to be pictured nine inches tall on a 14" × 22" FRAVER showcard. Dreams come true indeed. I don't think Frank had met a twenty-seven-year-old so obsessed with his work, so he took me to his office a few blocks away, and showed me some of his favorite pieces he had done over the years. I could only imagine then . . . "you should have a book or website of all your work." The website came a few years ago, and finally we have the book! He even did a mock-up of a poster for me for my birthday. I'm honored to call Frank a friend.

Today, I have a three-year-old named Georgia, and I'm on Broadway now in *Charlie and the Chocolate Factory*, so all my posters are tucked safely away in an air conditioned storage unit. But one day, I won't live in a tiny NYC apartment, and I can put up all my FRAVERS and exclaim á la Sweeney Todd, "At last my wall is complete again!"

I was very much inspired by turn-of-the-century illustrator Alphonse Mucha, who had designed some of the first and finest theatre poster art. He was Sarah Bernhardt's artist-of-record. I focused on the glamorous character of Desirée Armfeldt, who is the catalyst for all the romantic action, seated on a half-moon (circles again), amidst a sea of stars.

Company (2002)

Both the original production and the 1995 revival of this musical were represented by stunning logo designs. I felt it was time to humanize this show with an image. I purchased and photographed wedding cake figurines. My husband Joe Ligammari made the cake upon which Bobby and his potential brides reside. The production had a definite 1970s feel, hence the op-art background of circles. Actor John Barrowman was tremendous in the lead and was indeed a real doll.

Merrily We Roll Along (2002)

Since the clever device of this musical is to tell the story of three friends in reverse chronological order, I landed on the idea of photographing the main characters watching a sunrise— or is it a sunset? Broadway show jackets were all the rage and a favorite opening night gift in the 1980s. I own several to prove it, and thought it fitting to present the embroidered title logo as a nod to the date of the original production.

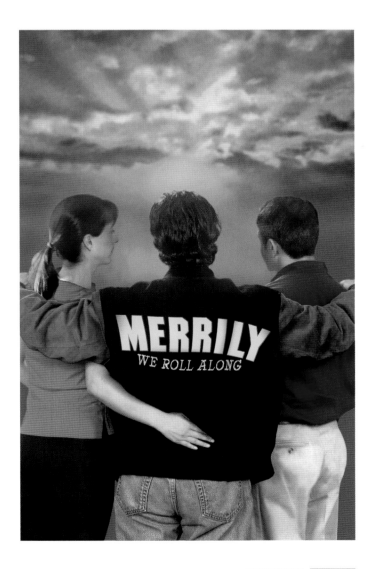

Pacific Overtures (2002)

Since I had created the art for the Off-Broadway revival in 1984, I decided this go-round to involve the same elements but scramble them up and use them in a completely different way. This is the only production of the entire Celebration I did not get to see. The performance schedule was a tricky one, and I unfortunately couldn't get to DC when it was playing.

Sunday in the Park with George (2002)

This was one of the three concepts I had presented for the original Broadway production. I always liked it and felt it was a strong solution to this musical challenge. Back then, I designed it as a graphic and the original was given to Mr. Sondheim as a gift. This time, I decided to treat it with realism. I scanned the paintbrush that I had smeared with acrylics and added the Seurat image in Photoshop.

Sweeney Todd (2002)

Talk about a challenge! My drawing of Sweeney and Mrs. Lovett for the original Broadway production had by now become "embedded into the very fabric of the show itself," as one writer put it. Needless to say, I decided to stay away from depicting the main characters. Instead, I chose to symbolize them. A hand-painted barber pole with a protective, squawking crow perched atop it captured the spirit of the show to me. Of the nine posters I designed for this Kennedy Center Celebration, Mr. Sondheim phoned me one day to discuss this one in particular. He wanted to know why I felt this art was appropriate for *Sweeney Todd*. We discussed it for quite some time. It is my experience that Mr. Sondheim is always willing to listen to the rationale behind a creative/design choice. By the end of our conversation, he gave me his blessing to go with it.

Passion (2002)

I felt this dark and intense musical needed a dark and intense image, hence the staring gaze of the main character, Fosca. Reflected in her eye is the object of her obsession, Giorgio. This was a brilliant production starring the amazing Judy Kuhn, whose glorious voice was perfect for the lush score. It also gave me a chance to design for a musical that I love more and more each time I see and hear it.

Pacific Overtures

THE SHUBERT ORGANIZATION
McCANN & NUGENT
present

PACIFIC OVERTURES

Music & Lyrics by   Book by
STEPHEN SONDHEIM   **JOHN WEIDMAN**

Additional Material by
HUGH WHEELER

Originally Directed and Produced by
HAROLD PRINCE

Scenery Designed by   Lighting Designed by   Costumes Designed by   Additional Costumes by
JAMES MORGAN   **MARY JO DONDLINGER**   **MARK PASSERELL**   **EIKO YAMAGUCHI**

Musical Director   Orchestrations by   Originally Choreographed by   Choreographer
ERIC STERN   **JAMES STENBORG**   **PATRICIA BIRCH**   **JANET WATSON**

Directed by
FRAN SOEDER

This production based on the March, 1984 York Theatre Company production,
Janet Hayes Walker, Producing Director.

PROMENADE THEATRE 2162 Broadway at 76th Street

Pacific Overtures (1984)

This was a much-anticipated first revival (Off-Broadway, directed by Fran Soeder) of one of Stephen Sondheim's incredible musicals. As with any project of this stature, many pieces of poster art were presented. In the end, producers Liz McCann and the Shubert Organization favored this simple line drawing based on a Japanese print. The Metropolitan Opera caught sight of it and commissioned me to design some pieces in the same style for sale in their gift shop. I designed posters for *Aida, Madame Butterfly, Samson and Delilah,* and *Pagliacci.* Unfortunately, they deemed the project "too expensive to produce" and it all fell by the wayside. However, it was fun working on them!

BERT FINK
CHIEF CREATIVE OFFICER, PROFESSIONAL LICENSING AT MTI

I was a fan of Fraver's long before I was lucky enough to work with Frank Verlizzo, since I kept noticing that sobriquet, "Fraver," penned into some especially witty and artful theatre posters.

So, by early 1984, when I was an assistant in the Fred Nathan Publicity Office, about to work on the Broadway premiere of *Sunday in the Park with George*, I was thrilled that I got to meet one of my heroes—who quickly became a colleague, and a lifelong friend. Fraver's logo for *Sunday in the Park* was a perfect encapsulation of its century-spanning duality, wholly original yet with just enough of an homage to Georges Seurat.

Having created instant-classic icons for both *Sweeney Todd* and *Sunday*, it was inevitable that Fraver would be tapped by author Craig Zadan when it was time to reissue Zadan's landmark book *Sondheim & Co.* Fraver leapt to the challenge and came up with various options for a new cover. (One design, alas not used, featured a version of the *New York Times'* theatre listings—the so-called A-B-C's —with every show a Sondheim musical. It boggled the mind!)

One day, Fraver sent over another idea for the cover —and I knew this was it: an elegant, tuxedoed torso (that of Fraver's elegant husband, Joe) with show buttons festooned on the sleek black lapel. It was the perfect combination of class and wit that made the cover an ideal match for its subject inside.

Working with Fraver, I understood how much detail he put into seemingly small decisions. A particular use of color, a certain brush stroke or textile, a tint of a photograph, was not perfect by happenstance; it was preceded by lots of thought and contemplation. And here's an example . . .

As detailed elsewhere in these pages, I had the pleasure of working with Fraver during my years at Rodgers & Hammerstein, when visionary leader Ted Chapin wanted to give the long-established catalogue a new and unified look. In the late '80s, Fraver created the R&H logo that is still in use to this day. In the early '90s, he created a series of songbook covers of the R&H shows that worked individually, and complemented each other as a series. And then, just after 2000, we turned to Fraver yet again, this time to create a logo for the *Richard Rodgers Centennial of 2002*. Not unlike his R&H logo (in which the ampersand was a G clef), here Fraver wove text with musical motifs, in this case using a quarter note as the stem of the R, and also using the alliteration of Richard Rodgers to patterned effect.

I remember asking Fraver how he came up with this idea. We were sitting in my office, where I had a copy of Rodgers' autobiography, *Musical Stages*, on my desk. Fraver pointed to Rodgers' signature, imprinted on the inside cover. "I was looking for clues, studying his signature," he said, "and I noticed that, in his own handwriting, the loop of the first 'R' is a sort of a '2', and it just clicked from there."

I looked again at a signature I had looked at a thousand times before. Only now, I was seeing it a whole new way. And that was thanks to Frank "Fraver" Verlizzo.

London, 2017

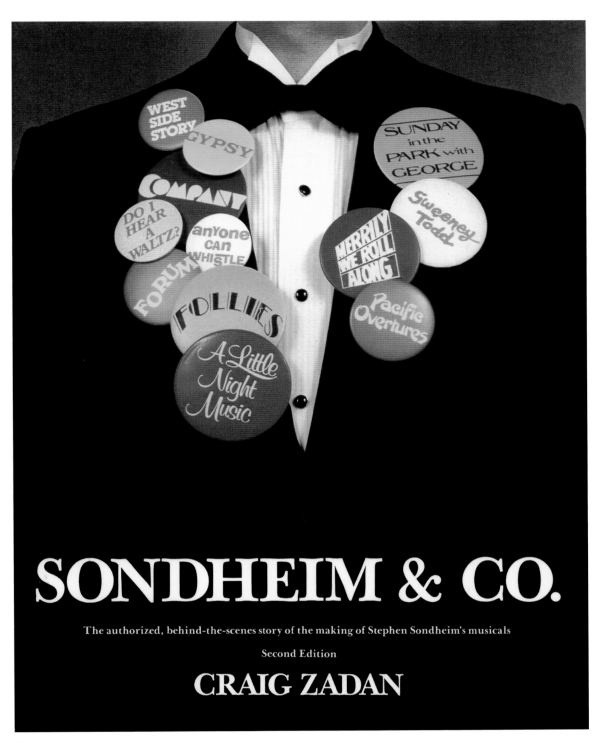

SONDHEIM & CO.

The authorized, behind-the-scenes story of the making of Stephen Sondheim's musicals

Second Edition

CRAIG ZADAN

Photography by John Reilly

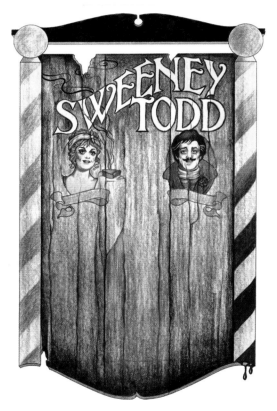

How exciting was it to work on one of the most celebrated musicals ever written? Absolutely incredibly exciting! Once again, a legion of art directors and designers were on hand to make our presentation at J. Walter Thompson Entertainment a spectacular event. After seeing nearly (I'm not joking) one hundred concepts, the favorites came down to another artist's silhouette graphic of Mrs. Lovett and Sweeney with their heads chopped off and my drawing. My *Sweeney* art was based on an old woodcut and I added Mrs. Lovett drawn in the same style. I had met with Harold Prince who showed me costume sketches in which the Mrs. Lovett character appeared very fat. He explained he was going to talk to his star about wearing padding but hadn't yet. My initial thought for Mrs. Lovett was the Queen of Hearts. I drew a hefty-bodied version that was a cross between John Tenniel's *Alice in Wonderland* drawings and Franne Lee's costume sketches. Angela Lansbury was just back from Egypt where she had finished filming *Death on the Nile*. I was asked to go to her apartment to show her the artwork so she could approve it. I fortunately thought to render other Mrs. Lovetts in various weights ranging from obese to svelt. Ms. Lansbury couldn't have been nicer but was taken aback by the girth of some of my renderings. I told her I'd heard mentioned the possibility of her wearing a "fat suit." Without missing a beat, her response was, "I'll just play it fat. Let's go with the thinnest drawing." The final suggestion Stephen Sondheim made: "Add more blood."

RICHARD BARR   CHARLES WOODWARD
ROBERT FRYER   MARY LEA JOHNSON   MARTIN RICHARDS
PRESENT

ANGELA LANSBURY   LEN CARIOU

IN

Sweeney Todd
The Demon Barber of Fleet Street

A MUSICAL THRILLER

MUSIC AND LYRICS BY
STEPHEN SONDHEIM

BOOK BY
HUGH WHEELER

BASED ON A VERSION OF "SWEENEY TODD" BY CHRISTOPHER BOND

DIRECTED BY
HAROLD PRINCE

PRODUCTION DESIGNED BY
EUGENE LEE

COSTUMES DESIGNED BY
FRANNE LEE

LIGHTING DESIGNED BY
KEN BILLINGTON

ORCHESTRATIONS BY
JONATHAN TUNICK

MUSICAL DIRECTOR
PAUL GEMIGNANI

DANCE AND MOVEMENT BY **LARRY FULLER**

ASSOCIATE PRODUCERS
DEAN & JUDY MANOS

ASSISTANT TO MR. PRINCE
RUTH MITCHELL

Original Broadway Cast Recording on **RCA** Records and Tapes

URIS THEATRE
50th STREET WEST OF BROADWAY

CHAPTER THREE

RODGERS & HAMMERSTEIN

The King and I (2012)

This has long been my favorite musical of all time! It's set in an exotic locale, has shimmering costumes (glitter is my favorite color), an incomparable score, a cast of thousands (or so it seems), all the mystery and romance anyone could ask for in a story—with the extra added bonus of featuring a leading man who rarely wears a shirt. This was my fourth in the R&H poster series. Dana Siegel, the marketing director, explained to me the goal of these posters: designed so that even without their title logos attached, a licensing client could identify the show. The secondary theory was to have the art contain the feel of a travel poster. Throughout *The King and I* theatre poster history, I always felt that the lead character of the schoolteacher was shortchanged. The focus is always on His Majesty. Here, I bring Mrs. Anna front and center along with a gilded symbol of Siam.

Courtesy of Rodgers & Hammerstein, an Imagem Company, www.rnh.com

TED CHAPIN
RODGERS & HAMMERSTEIN ORGANIZATION

It was Bert Fink who introduced me to the person behind "Fraver."

We at Rodgers & Hammerstein had been operating with a logo and stationery that looked like someone had thrown together some cheap lettering during the 1950s and taken it to a printer. Bert suggested I meet Frank to see if he had ideas for a logo, and a look that might bring the perception of who we were more up-to-date. Although both Rodgers and Hammerstein were long gone, the office had good theatrical energy and our task was to keep the shows alive in and for the modern world.

I don't remember conversations, or even if there were conversations, before the three of us met for lunch when Frank was going to present us with two ideas. The first was on a board, an image of the two men artfully manipulated so as not to be photographic, along with some music staff lines and the words "Rodgers & Hammerstein" in a lovely script. Well, I thought, it is certainly "a look." A little busy and complicated, perhaps. Then, if memory serves, Frank said that while he liked it (I think this is one of his secrets—if he says he likes everything, then he can get a more honest reaction from the client) perhaps we could do something a little simpler. Out from his bag he took a grey/brown coffee mug on which he had appliquéd "R&H," the two letters bold but flowing, the ampersand made from a G clef, intertwining the two letters to make them belong together as one clear, focused unit. Done. Simple, artful, and so appropriate to our situation: from nothing, we had a look. And it said the right thing.

Rodgers and Hammerstein wrote their shows in a pretty graphic-free, or at least graphically unsophisticated, era. The original productions all had posters. They were mostly lettering, without iconic images that branded the shows. So years later we handed Frank a different task: create for us, the poster art that people think was always in existence for *Oklahoma!*, *The Sound of Music*, *South Pacific*, etc.

This wasn't as easy as the logo—but Frank approached it with the tact of a psychiatrist, (there were more of us with opinions this time around) and the skill of a negotiator. This clearly reflected the experience of someone who had been through the Broadway ringer, and, of course, his own intrinsic talent.

On his tablet, he could flip a finger to move from one idea to the next. And at each new image, he listened carefully. His opinions were given gently, and by the end of each session, I had a pretty good sense of where he thought we should head. (Truth is, I always enjoy quiet sidebars with him . . .) Some took a few tries, but the results are great, and we're very proud of them.

I love working with Frank. He's a great artist.

Courtesy of Rodgers & Hammerstein, an Imagem Company, www.rnh.com

Who, at one time or another, didn't want to meet or to be Dream Curly? With *Oklahoma!*, the same rules applied to my second show design project for R&H: easily identifiable without title while possessing the feel of a travel poster. Using a field of wheat, a windmill, a hat, and a flower, this art pretty much created itself! I do find the results strikingly handsome and musical theatre-worthy.

Courtesy of Rodgers & Hammerstein, an Imagem Company, www.rnh.com

As a kid, I played the original cast recording of *South Pacific* ad nauseam. For my third R&H artwork assignment, I enlisted all the familiar images relating to that Pulitzer Prize-winning show. Adventure and romance were my guides in using the fighter planes and discarded lei as the focal points. I used bright, highly saturated colors to lend an otherworldly tone to both the time and place.

Courtesy of Rodgers & Hammerstein, an Imagem Company, www.rnh.com

"The Carousel Waltz" is one of my top ten favorite pieces of theatre music. It embodies all the glitter and grandeur anyone could ask for from the art form. I was asked by Ted Chapin of R&H to use the most familiar elements of the story—lighthouse, water, stars, and a carousel horse—in approaching my designs. I feel this colorful, expressive, sculpted creature conveys the essence of what makes the show so dramatic. To date, I've designed the "official" R&H posters for six of their classic musicals. I'm hoping one day to be able to tackle *Flower Drum Song* as well!

Courtesy of Rodgers & Hammerstein, an Imagem Company, www.rnh.com

The names Rodgers & Hammerstein were always magical to me. In my mind, R&H were synonymous with Broadway musicals. When I was hired by R&H to create their corporate logo, we briefly discussed having me design the "official" posters to be used in their licensing. Great things happen to those who wait! They chose *The Sound of Music* as the first project and asked me to design it. Aside from an expansive sky and the Alps, which were a given, I chose to focus on the seven budding edelweiss as the foreground: one for each of the von Trapp children.

4

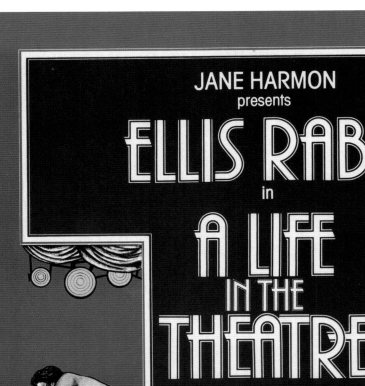

JANE HARMON

presents

ELLIS RABB

in

A LIFE IN THE THEATRE

By
DAVID MAMET

With
PETER EVANS

Scenery by	Lighting by	Costumes by
JOHN LEE BEATTY	**PAT COLLINS**	**JOHN DAVID RIDGE**

Incidental Music by
ROBERT WALDMAN

Directed by
GERALD GUTIERREZ

THEATRE DE LYS
121 Christopher Street / WA 4-8782

FRAVER

A Life in the Theatre (1977)

I am often asked if I design differently for Broadway and Off-Broadway. One answer is that my creative choices usually rely on the production's budgetary allotment for print media buying. Years before technology entered the theatre scene, the advertising resources would dictate whether the artwork would be 4-color, 3-color, 2-color, or black and white. Show biz professionals could usually determine a Broadway from an Off-Broadway production based solely on the money spent printing the window card and show flyers. Today, with digital alternatives, it's all affordable. The choice of using 4-color or black and white is simply a design decision made by the poster artist.

Another answer to the question of designing for Off-Broadway versus Broadway involves less of a formula and more of an aesthetic vibe. I do tend toward edgier concepts when creating for an Off-Broadway production. Or maybe, after all, it is an antiquated query since technology has leveled the budgetary playing field somewhat. Current Off-Broadway shows can afford the same 4-color online e-mail blast that a prominent Broadway show can. Some of the various avenues of media buying, however, are cost-prohibitive to most smaller Off-Broadway productions, a good example being direct mail.

I treat every new project, either Broadway or Off-Broadway, as if it's going to be the next big thing. I love diving into scripts, but I'd hardly call myself a good barometer for judging their success potential. I've read great plays that later bombed on stage and vice versa. My job is to generate an arresting image, whatever the vehicle, and create a poster intriguing enough to warrant a second look, and ultimately, to entice a potential ticket buyer to seek out more information.

The art presentation typically involves many people from the assorted departments of the production. An average meeting would include the producers, the general manager, the press agent, the creative/art director, the ad agency account executive, the ad agency copywriter, the show's company manager, and various assistants from these offices. I've presented artwork for a new show in meetings with as few as six people to seismic events of twenty attendees or more! The producer generally sets the bar for how many opinions he or she wants in the room. For diplomatic reasons, or contractual ones, the playwright, composer, and/or director might join the group as well.

What follows is basically a two-dimensional beauty contest disguised as a marketing meeting. Before the action gets into full swing, I usually spend my time evaluating the climate of the mix of people in the room. Sometimes it's obvious to me who the absolute decisionmakers are, other times, not so much. If it's a group I've worked with before on other shows, that makes sizing things up a bit easier. However, in a fresh configuration, although comprised of some of the same people I may know from other shows, they are now tossed into a new chemistry with other players who may be unfamiliar to them. As within any assembled group, some people can easily get along with others while others might need some cajoling.

In my time presenting poster art, there have been instances of producers accompanied by gun-toting bodyguards, clients expert at theatrical histrionics demonstrating their prowess, pleasant groups in which no one wants to take responsibility for a design decision, unpleasant groups who slug it out for hours until the third-choice poster is the piece crowned because it's the only one everyone can agree upon, and one instance of a drunken producer who fell over backwards in his chair much to everyone's horror and amusement. But even he managed to weigh in on the artwork.

Anyone with eyes is a theatre poster critic. Guiding any group of people to nod their heads in accord is difficult, much less to get them to agree on a piece of art that must serve to function as 1) a strong advertising tool, 2) valuable merchandising material, and 3) framed artwork for the benefit of home decor.

After the poster is chosen, the collaboration process begins. Up until that point, I pretty much have had free reign on my design concepts, color choices, type designs, fonts, etc. Now, I must collect all of the opinions and critiques and make desired revisions. A week or two later, we then hold a subsequent gathering to present the amended poster art. I generally create many variations, each of them slightly different, incorporating the design alterations requested by the client unit in regard to color, logo, and concept. Sometimes it's a fun exercise retooling artwork, other times, it's agony. Whatever the process, there's always something of value I learn from the exercise.

That is part of my job. And I love it.

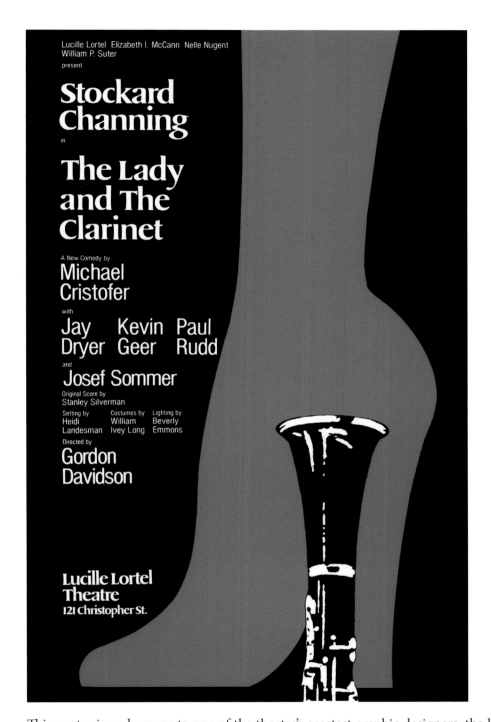

This poster is an homage to one of the theatre's greatest graphic designers, the late Gilbert Lesser. He used very simple shapes and bold color in very arresting ways in all of his work. Gil was responsible for some of the most beautiful theatre poster art in the '70s and '80s, including *Equus*, *The Elephant Man*, and the short-lived extravaganza *Frankenstein*. He was a frequent visitor to our Blaine Thompson offices and would laughingly tell people he "taught me how to cut paper." Once again, I chose red, black, and white as the palette. The concept here was using the titular musical instrument as the trompe l'oeil negative space in the red high heel shoe. This poster was a Clio Award finalist.

Photography by Joan Marcus

This one-man play by Jonathan Tolins was a surprise hit garnering unanimous rave reviews and ecstatic audience word-of-mouth. The run began at Rattlestick Theatre in Greenwich Village and later moved slightly further downtown to Barrow Street Theatre. The star, Michael Urie, gives a Drama Desk Award-winning performance as an aspiring actor who lands a job as the only vendor in Barbra Streisand's otherwise uninhabited private mall. The producers were giving the show a much-deserved extended run in a bigger Off-Broadway venue and asked me to see it before it ended at Rattlestick. My first thought was to parody some famous Streisand poster images. One from the Broadway show *Funny Girl* (remember my first boss, Morris Robbins, designed the original) and the film *Funny Lady*. When that notion didn't fly with the producers, I knew it was best to keep it simple. The play has one lovely set, mostly white, with some projections. We had a fun photo shoot with the fantastic Joan Marcus to replace the "comp" Michael Urie and I had used as a placeholder in my early poster version. The upper case B in the final artwork is a jazzed-up, marquee-type version of the font that Ms. Streisand typically employs on her album covers.

SCOTT MORFEE
FOUNDING PRODUCER OF BARROW STREET THEATRE

When marketing a show, the two urgent challenges upon which all is built are the blurb—an economical written description—and the art, which provides instant, and hopefully memorable, visual identity to the entire enterprise. In retrospect, having revisited the artwork for the productions involving Frank Verlizzo (and that is a lot), I noticed that we have been virtually all-graphic, not employing any photography, which, for many, is a valid alternative or a long-term artistic choice. The second observation—and I admit that this is all somewhat subliminal—is that our shows generally worked within a scheme of colors, primarily red, black, white, with an occasional lean towards yellow/gold.

Show artwork is satisfactory when it cleanly communicates the title, but the really good stuff, to me, also conveys something more, stimulates some other part of the brain. When presented with many artistic options for a show's key artwork, it is virtually always the one treatment that generates the most debate in our group that ultimately wins. In the artwork for *Our Town,* it's the "O" as the moon that moves the needle; it is subtle, peaceful, and notes Wilder's fascination with the sun, the moon, and the stars—all major elements in his masterful play.

For *Adding Machine,* please note the playful color scheme, where the art is made transcendent by the addition of a simple splash of very red blood.

His art for *Hit the Wall* managed to convey so much that it needs to be delineated: it is part map of a neighborhood, a time and place marked within—"Stonewall," and part homage to the historic pink triangle of Act Up. When "assembled" the artwork represents the location of the movement that was inspired by that one frenzied weekend, in that neighborhood, and on that spot. The art is chaotic, jarring, ACTIVE! Brilliant.

For *Cymbeline,* remove the title; what remains is a very complex layering of that specific production. The play is about marital intrigue and betrayal and the royals and, well, it is Shakespeare, so why catalog THAT entire list? But, the art features a ring, and a royal learning what it means to be "lopped-off." Look closer—the hand is also a musical instrument, our production was musicalized and included a French Horn; and oh, please count the fingers. Intrigue!

Besides the fact that I love op-art, I admit I was not initially convinced that *The Effect's* artwork was the right choice. But then a lightbulb went off one day, and now I cannot believe that we deliberated as we did. *The Effect* is a play about clinical studies for depression drugs and the placebo effect. It challenges clinical protocols and riddles the audience with questions about what exactly is real when it comes to human emotion—especially when it is "possibly" medicated. The artwork is boldly about perception, and it briefly tricks both the eye and the mind. It is the title of the play, sort of; just takes a moment to process. Good art will earn that extra moment, no matter the color scheme.

Our Town (2009)

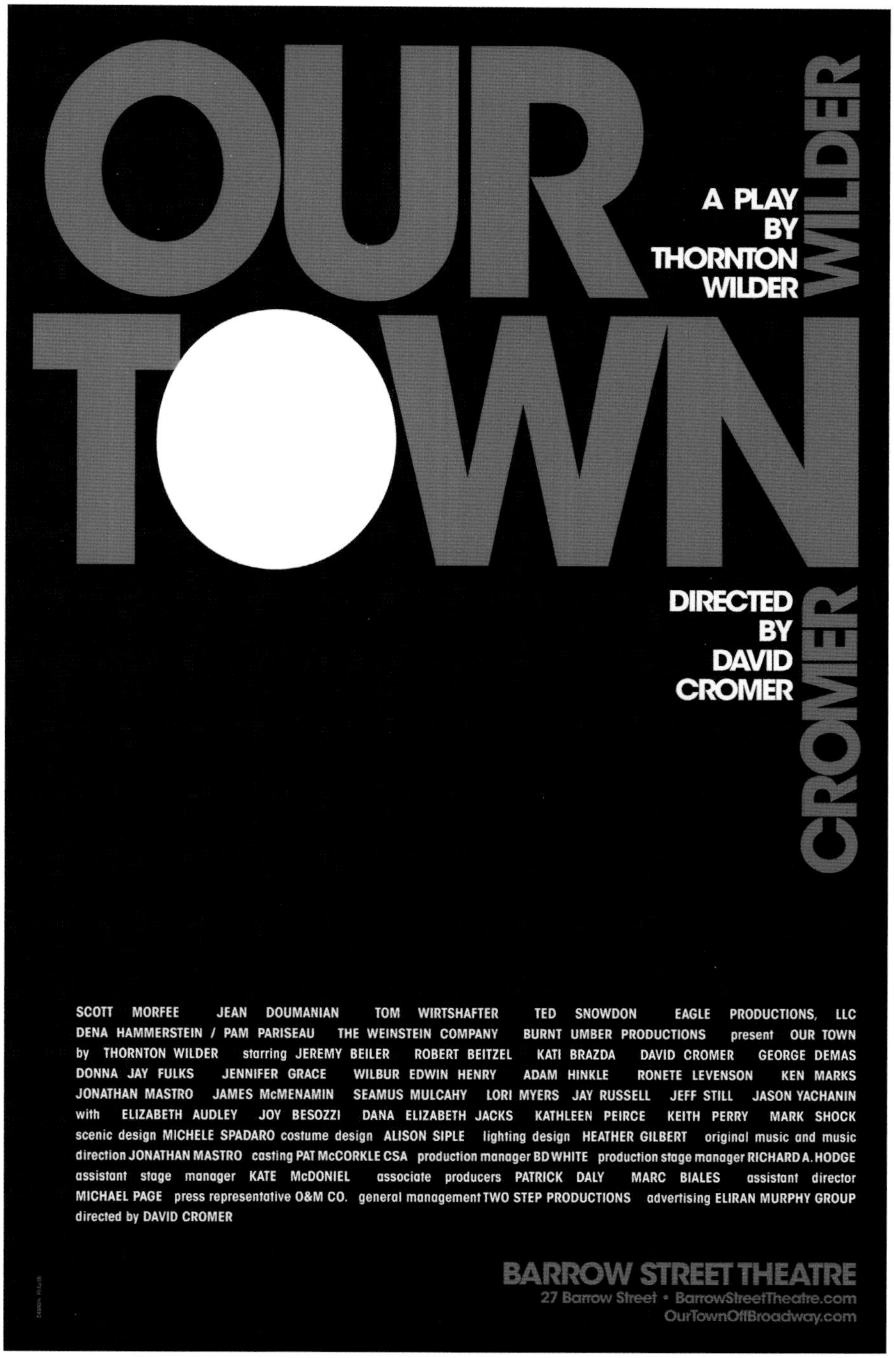

JEAN DOUMANIAN
THEATRE, TELEVISION, AND FILM PRODUCER

A poster is, at its heart, a sales tool. It is the public face of any production, and as such it needs to entice and engage a potential audience. But a great poster is also a piece of art. It should catch your eye and draw you in. It should invoke an emotional response and invite the viewer to want to learn more. There are many people who can make sales tools; Frank Verlizzo makes art.

I have had the privilege of working with Frank on a number of productions. His many designs have impressed and thrilled me, but the consistent standout in each poster he has designed for me is the title treatment. Each title treatment is unique and evocative and, while the typography may be simple and pure, each makes a clear artistic statement. From the striking and inviting white "O" in the *Our Town* poster, to the enigmatic block lettering of the psychologically dense *The Effect*, to the hand-drawn font for *Tribes*, each embodies subliminally and abstractly the intent of the play. A poster does not need to explain the plot; it just needs to create the beacon that compels an audience to attend and even retain the image of the poster long after the experience of the play.

My plays would not be the same without Frank's posters. They have become an integral part of each production. Frank is an artist whose work elevates and illuminates the shows they represent.

National Theatre

THE EFFECT

A new play by **Lucy Prebble** Directed by **David Cromer**

**BARROW
STREET
THEATRE**

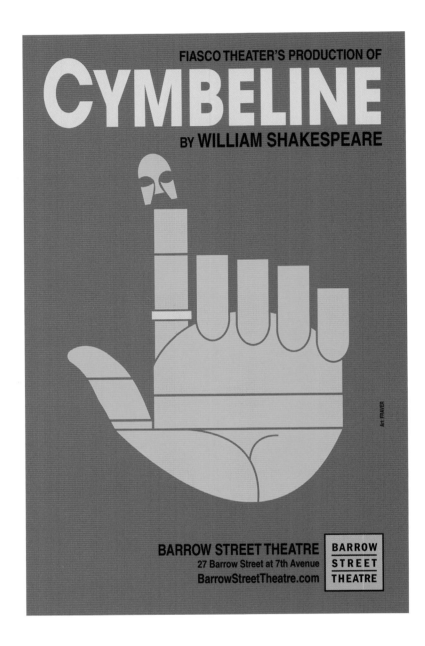

It is always a special occasion when I am asked to design for a Scott Morfee, Jean Doumanian, and Tom Wirtshafter production. On this go-round, they were teaming up with Fiasco Theatre to re-mount their earlier workshop of *Cymbeline*. Of course, it would be staged at Barrow Street Theatre. This play, like many other of Shakespeare's, tells a very convoluted story involving kings, queens, and those in line for a throne. Throw in some country folk, a ring, a bracelet, a beheading, mistaken identity, and a miraculously simple box (the only real stage prop for this show) and you start to get a sense of the broad plot line. I wanted to design a strong, bold graphic image that could be seen from a block away. The poster depicts the ticking off of the various characters in line for the throne, hopefully in a humorous and attractive way. Presented on a bare-bones budget, one of the remarkable aspects of this *Cymbeline* was that it had a cast of six playing the numerous characters. Thus, the hand has six fingers.

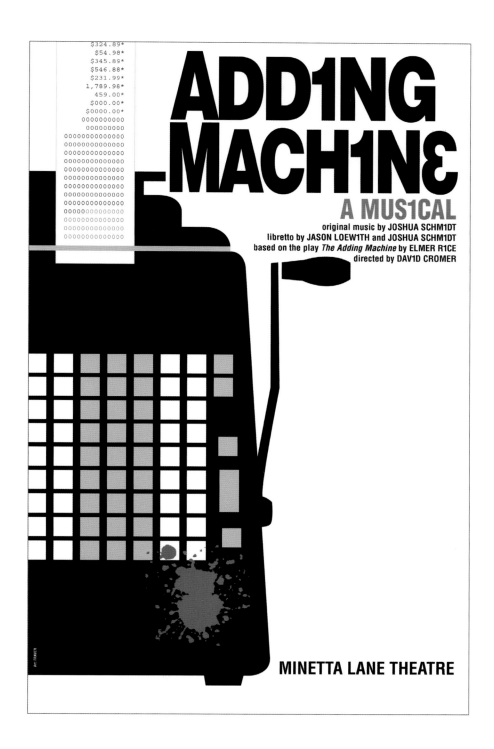

Presenting this David Cromer-directed chamber musical was definitely a daring enterprise. Once again, producer Scott Morfee and crew garnered rave reviews and many awards for this innovative theatre piece. It's a heavy show about eternity, love, murder, etc. I chose to use the titular period piece of machinery as our image. Press agents Rick Miramontez and Jon Dimond strongly supported my belief that this dark period piece needed a crisp contemporary graphic.

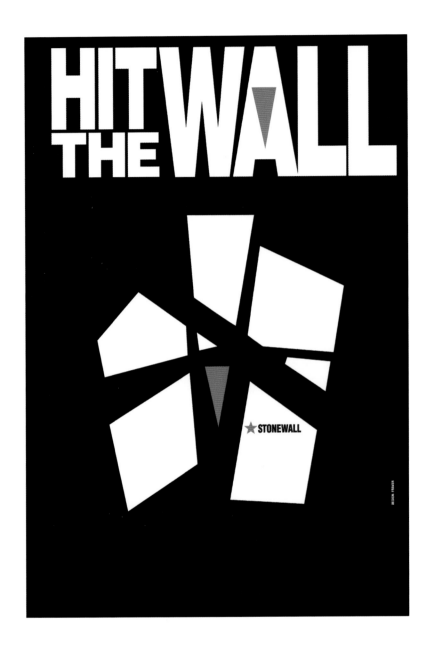

Producers Scott Morfee, Jean Doumanian, and Tom Wirtshafter are the dream team behind all the recent hit plays presented at Barrow Street Theatre. I have had the pleasure of working with them for years, counting *Our Town* and *Tribes* among their shows to garner awards and rave reviews (and enthusiastic audiences!). *Hit the Wall* is a play that received wonderful acclaim and word-of-mouth from its run at the Steppenwolf Garage in Chicago. As with most shows, I met with the producers early on to discuss their thoughts regarding the poster art. One of the remarks that stayed with me later, while designing, was how important the geography of Greenwich Village was to the Stonewall Inn story. I took the idea of a map (something I always find very difficult to follow) and created basic shapes of the streets that ultimately looked like shattered glass. Using the design elements of triangular Christopher Park as the central focus and a star to designate Stonewall across the street from it, I hope this poster captures the vibrant nature of *Hit the Wall* and its representation of an important time in history.

IN 59 MINUTES
WE WILL TAKE YOU
RIGHT TO THE EDGE.

BEIRUT

desire   denial

Westside Arts Theatre

Photography by Carol Rosegg

Actress Laura San Giacomo had just been cast and was flying into NYC just in time for our scheduled photo session. She was joining fellow actor Michael David Morrison, who had starred in a previous incarnation. I had a rough sketch (already approved by our producers) of what we were going to shoot: two naked people in a fierce embrace, which I would later work into an inverted graphic triangle. Carol Rosegg was the photographer and we were all set up, waiting for Ms. San Giacomo to arrive from the airport. She showed up in a flurry, apologized for a delayed cab ride and said, "What are we shooting?" I asked, "Did you not see the concept sketch?" "No . . . they just cast me yesterday." I must say, she lost all color in her face when she realized she had to pose with her co-star completely naked. But she was a trooper, and the brilliant Rosegg photo works beautifully.

The Acting Company: *Macbeth* and *A Connecticut Yankee in King Arthur's Court* (2015)

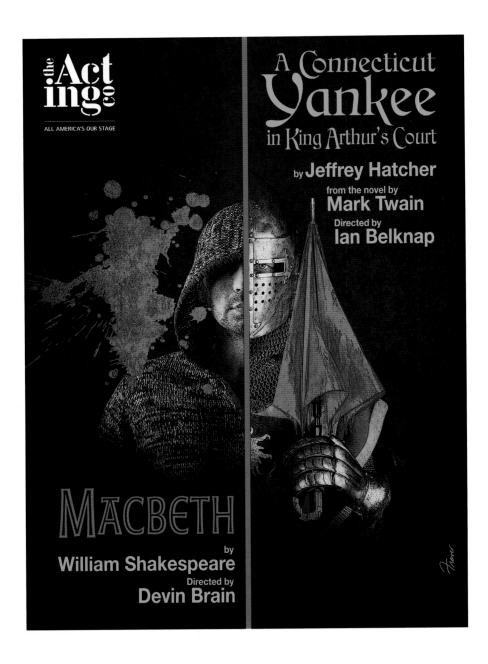

When first asked to design their season art, the challenge was to create one poster for two productions. Since it turned out to be a success, the request once again came to have a single poster represent both *Macbeth* and *A Connecticut Yankee in King Arthur's Court*. This time, I designed in a vertical format, splitting the poster directly at the center. The colors are muted except for the bright red blood spatter in Shakespeare's masterpiece and the red umbrella for Twain's. I was pleased with the results and TAC's Ian Belknap and Gerry Cornez were very enthusiastic about it as well!

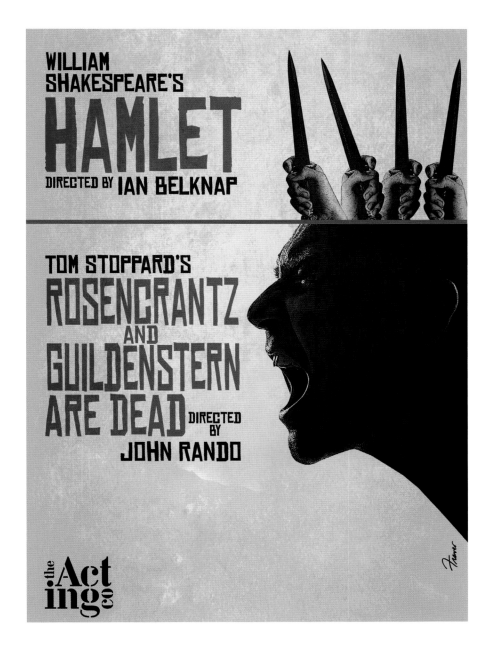

It's a great honor for me to finally have gotten the opportunity to work with this illustrious theatre group! I met with the new artistic director, Ian Belknap. It also gave me a chance to catch up with Gerry Cornez, a wonderful friend who always has the best theatre stories to share. For their 2013–14 season, TAC was presenting *Hamlet* and Tom Stoppard's *Rosencrantz and Guildenstern Are Dead* in repertory. Ian and Gerry requested that the art for both shows be designed as one poster and work as a unit. They initially asked for an all-type solution. That's one of my favorite challenges since I studied typography at Pratt Institute. I did present some type-only solutions but decided that I would also show an image poster as well. This was the one they chose!

GERARD ALESSANDRINI
PLAYWRIGHT, PARODIST, ACTOR, AND STAGE DIRECTOR

As a theatre director and writer, I've always felt that a show poster designer is crucially important to a production. The designer must possess unique and multiple talents. Not only does he have to be a superb artist but he also has to be a great showman. A successful show poster has to perform as well as inform. The designer is a collaborator and even a cast member. It takes a very specialized brilliance to accomplish both. Fraver is exactly that type of talent.

In the case of our *Forbidden Broadway* revues, the show is constantly changing, so we need the logo and poster to evolve depending on the edition. We need a fresh and eyebrow-raising look, yet at the same time we need to refer to the brand's logo. It's like wanting our cake and eating it too. Fraver is always up to the challenge and delightfully surpasses our expectations.

His ideas for design and layout always get the comedic tone just right. Even though he creates various versions, each one hits the bull's eye. Sometimes it's hard to choose which design to use. He is always eager to help us discover the right tone of funny for each edition. He's tremendously accommodating, yet brilliant in coming up with fresh suggestions and ideas. As the show's creator, I couldn't ask for a better visual collaborator.

His sense of color, design, and comedy is unsurpassed, but more than that, I always find his designs for *Forbidden Broadway* (and other shows too) wonderfully surprising and even startlingly hilarious. And as a writer this is very reassuring because with a Fraver poster, I always know the laughs will start rolling with the first glance!

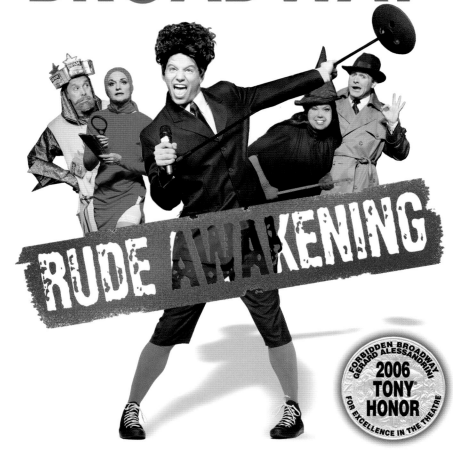

Photography by Carol Rosegg

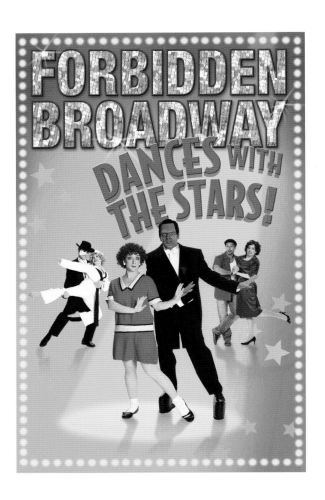

Forbidden Broadway
(2004–2008)

I've been fortunate to have worked on several editions of this legendary franchise. The *Rude Awakening* poster took the traditional look to a whole new level—actually spoofing the show art upon which this *Forbidden Broadway* edition was based. *Forbidden Broadway: Special Victims Unit* (2004) was one of the first posters in the series to use a strong concept to house the various Broadway show characters. I was especially thrilled because it gave me an opportunity to work with my talented friend, actor Jared Bradshaw, who just happens to be an avid musical theatre poster collector!

Photography by Carol Rosegg

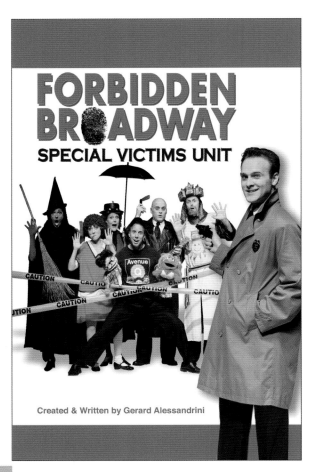

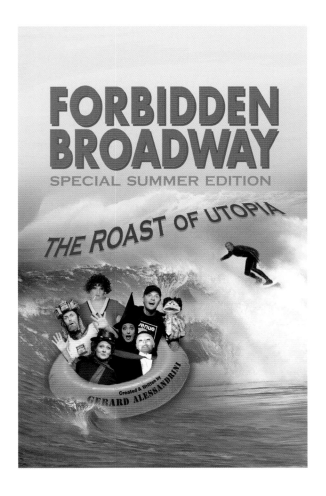

Photography by Jean-Marie Guyaux

I was a rabid fan of both TV's *Peyton Place* and the Roman Polanski film of Ira Levin's book *Rosemary's Baby*. So when Playwrights Horizons asked me to come up with concepts for photo set-ups with Mia Farrow, I'd never been more excited! Since I designed the shoot to be nearly prop-free and framed in tight close-up, photographer Jean-Marie Guyaux and I were asked to get the shot at Mia Farrow's Connecticut home. (Could an assignment get any better?) We spent a lovely day with the actress, who is radiantly beautiful in person, as well as being one of the warmest, most patient stars I've ever worked with. The photos were spectacular, but my favorite part of the day was when I found a few quiet moments to gossip and chat with Mia Farrow on a number of subjects ranging from Old Hollywood beauty secrets, retouched family albums, and Primo Levi! Oh, and the fan boy in me couldn't help but phone my brother to say "Guess what? I am calling you from Mia Farrow's bathroom!"

COMMENTARY

CLAUDIA SHEAR
PLAYWRIGHT AND ACTRESS

One of the purest most unalloyed joys of playwriting is seeing the poster.

Firstly, it's the knowledge that the production is actually happening, there is a theatre and an address and it is going to live! And then, and this is exponential in its delight if it's a Fraver . . . the poster. Because a Fraver is a design that illuminates the play you've written, Frank is attuned to every play he works on and all his posters reflect that. For example, when I saw his design for *Restoration,* a play I wrote based on the true story of one woman's restoring Michelangelo's *David*, the image was so evocative and romantic that I could only hope the play would live up to it. (The real life restorer cried when she saw it.)

I am just back from Paris, doing research for a new play and, in these first fumbling days in front of blank pages, maybe I will let myself imagine a moment, however far in the future, where Frank and I will sit and talk about the play I've written, a Fraver poster something devoutly to be wished, truly a goal to strive for.

And on a personal note, the loveliest and most gracious person ever, whose husband, Joe, makes the best martinis.

Photography by Joan Marcus

Playwright Patrick Barlow, who adapted Alfred Hitchcock's *The 39 Steps* for the stage, now had five actors bring to life all of Dickens' immortal characters, from Scrooge and Tiny Tim to Bob Cratchit and Mrs. Fezziwig, using nothing more than some simple props, fresh physicality, and the power of imagination. I wanted to create artwork for this merry version with something more exciting than the expected image of Tiny Tim perched on Scrooge's shoulder. It is a ghost story after all, so I thought having it look mystical and magical (and a bit creepy) was very appropriate. This production was also different in that it cast Scrooge as a handsome figure, which I thought was a great twist. I used him as the centerpiece of my poster design.

Paula Vogel's sprawling play (with music) freshly re-imagines a blustery Christmas Eve during the Civil War in 1864. It weaves fictional characters and historical figures in a kaleidoscopic tapestry. I was most struck by the thought of the first holiday tree and what it meant. Ornamented with images both happy and forlorn, in colors blue and grey, I hope this artwork captures a play that comes alive with history and humanity. The tree shape couldn't be more familiar. It's scanning through the disparate elements within the triangle that informs the piece.

Red Dog Howls (2012)

It was a thrill to be asked by New York Theatre Workshop to design the poster art for their 2012–13 season. This chilling play about buried family secrets, starring the formidable Kathleen Chalfant, was first up. Reading the script left me with a creepy feeling that I tried to capture with this imagery. Based on the reaction it received from the folks at NYTW at the art presentation, I think it was successful. It made them shudder—and they loved it!

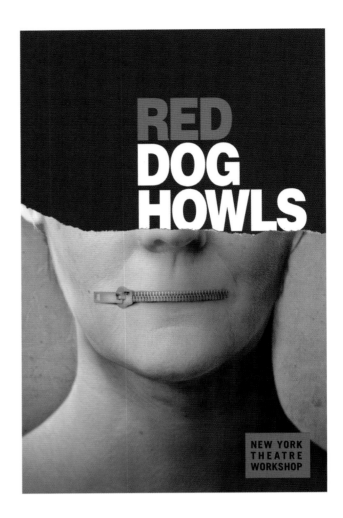

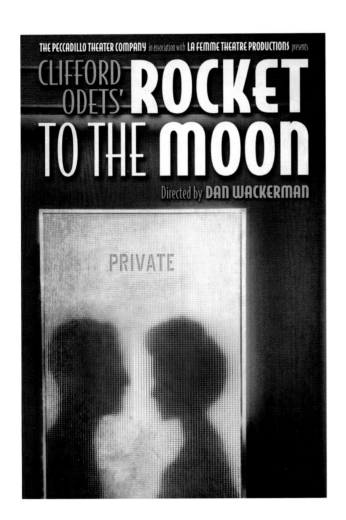

Rocket to the Moon (2015)

This rare revival, of the 1938 play by Clifford Odets (*Awake and Sing*, *Golden Boy*) was directed by Obie Award-winner Dan Wackerman. It was a great production filled with drama, sex, and humor. In doing research, I found most previous poster designs for the play used a literal rocket as a symbol. The "rocket to the moon" talked about in the play actually refers to having an illicit love affair. I took a different tact from the other designers and focused on the "private" office door—and catching two of the main characters perhaps about to embrace.

Cakewalk (1996)

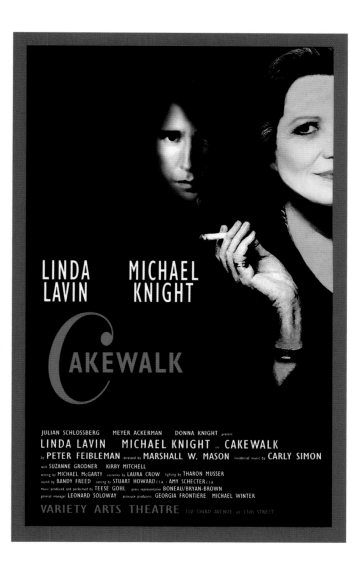

Actress Linda Lavin portraying playwright Lillian Hellman led me to immediately think *smoking*. In doing research, I rarely came across a photograph of Ms. Hellman without a cigarette in her hand. In my illustration, I used a vaporous image of actor Michael Knight as her younger lover and a half-visible portrait of Ms. Lavin that allowed me to feature both stars without one overpowering the other on the poster.

My Name Is Asher Lev (2012)

Producer Darren Bagert transferred this critically praised play, based on Chaim Potok's novel about a conflicted young artist, to Off-Broadway's Westside Theatre. In conversations early on, he and I discussed many design options. My takeaway from these talks was that Darren was very interested in exploring textures: paintbrush strokes, ice on a frozen windowpane, the effect of charcoal on drawing paper, etc. After numerous rounds and revisions, he landed on this paint-spattered portrait of the titular character. It proved to be very effective in all forms of media from online banners in full color to the *New York Times* print ad in black and white.

All the Rage (2012)

Martin Moran's show is a follow-up to his remarkable play *The Tricky Part*. Martin is one of the nicest, sweetest men I've ever met and I was very excited when he contacted me to design the poster art for his new production. It takes place in many geographical locations. The intricate story involves a childhood trauma, show business, political asylum, Pangaea, the *Origins of Man*, volunteering, and confronting anger issues. Needless to say, it's an intelligent, exciting story chock-full of imagery. In our first meeting, Martin told me that the ad agency had presented artwork to no avail. It was all too complicated, busy, and confusing. I always aim to break a show down to its simplest graphic message. This portrait of Martin as a puzzle being assembled, along with the background of passport stamps, really spoke to the creative team. The gorgeous photograph of the playwright is a composite of shots by the fantastic Joan Marcus.

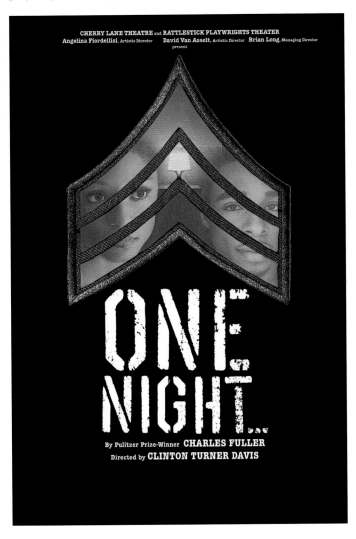

One Night . . . (2013)

Pulitzer Prize-winner Charles Fuller (*A Soldier's Play*) wrote a searing work about sexual harassment in the military. It was being produced by my friend Angelina Fiordellisi (Cherry Lane Theatre) and David Van Asselt (Rattlestick Theatre). They wanted to use their lead actress and actor's likenesses in the art. Typically, this is problematic for a show that is looking ahead to a longer life outside of the New York theatre scene. Once the cast starts to change, so must the art. It's standard practice that unless you're building the show on a certain star, you keep away from specific portraits. I was using the graphic device of sergeant stripes to encase the actors. The art was almost completely done when—you guessed it—there was a cast change. The new actress was Rutina Wesley from *True Blood*. The producers' request then became an advertising advantage!

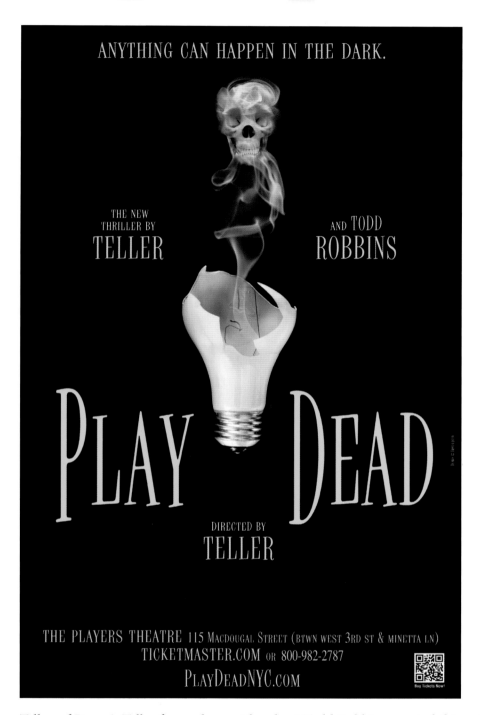

Teller, of Penn & Teller fame, along with cohort Todd Robbins, created this spirit-shaking show that explores themes of death, darkness, and deception. Audiences test their nerves and face their fears as they are surrounded by ethereal sights, sounds, and even touches of the returning dead—all achieved by wry, suspenseful storytelling and uncanny stage illusions. I met with producer Cheryl Wiesenfeld very early on. I think what impressed her most was my extensive knowledge of horror movies (love them!) and my enthusiasm about the very creepy subject matter. The light bulb image is very effective and evokes the essence of this fright-filled evening of pure theatre fun.

Fanny Hill (2006)

Multi-talented Ed Dixon wrote this charming musical based on John Cleland's notorious eighteenth-century erotic novel. The show has characters galore and was more elaborately produced than the usual fare at the York Theatre. The entire cast, lead by glorious Nancy Anderson, was extraordinary. It marked the first time I'd ever seen Tony Yazbeck on stage. He was a wonder to hear as well as to behold!

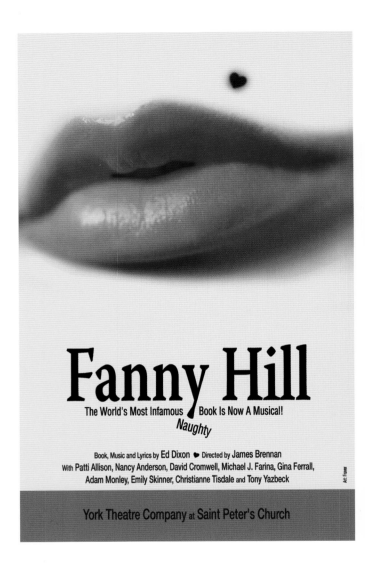

Fanny Hill

The World's Most Infamous / Book Is Now A Musical!
Naughty

Book, Music and Lyrics by Ed Dixon ● Directed by James Brennan
With Patti Allison, Nancy Anderson, David Cromwell, Michael J. Farina, Gina Ferrall,
Adam Monley, Emily Skinner, Christianne Tisdale and Tony Yazbeck

Art: Fraver

York Theatre Company at **Saint Peter's Church**

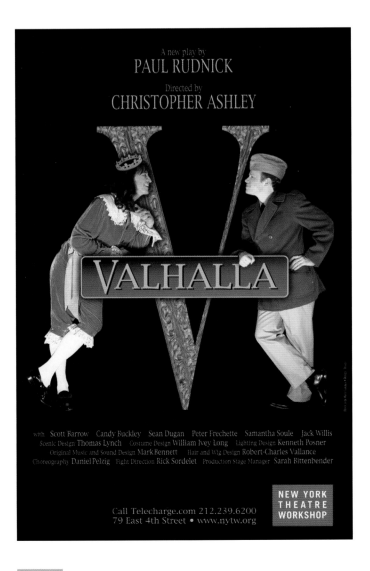

A new play by
PAUL RUDNICK

Directed by
CHRISTOPHER ASHLEY

VALHALLA

with Scott Barrow   Candy Buckley   Sean Dugan   Peter Frechette   Samantha Soule   Jack Willis
Scenic Design Thomas Lynch   Costume Design William Ivey Long   Lighting Design Kenneth Posner
Original Music and Sound Design Mark Bennett   Hair and Wig Design Robert-Charles Vallance
Choreography Daniel Pelzig   Fight Direction Rick Sordelet   Production Stage Manager Sarah Bittenbender

NEW YORK
THEATRE
WORKSHOP

Call Telecharge.com 212.239.6200
79 East 4th Street ● www.nytw.org

Valhalla (2004)

Paul Rudnick's brilliant play covered a lot of territory and two periods of time, which made for a design challenge. The main characters were mad King Ludwig II in 1860 and a sex-crazed 1940s juvenile delinquent who joins the army. I merged both worlds by connecting the two characters with a gilt "V" and a lozenge-shaped bridge, which contains the play title, on which both men are leaning. Jean-Marie Guyaux shot the beautiful photography based on my idea of using Maxfield Parrish storybook lighting and color.

Photography by Jean-Marie Guyaux

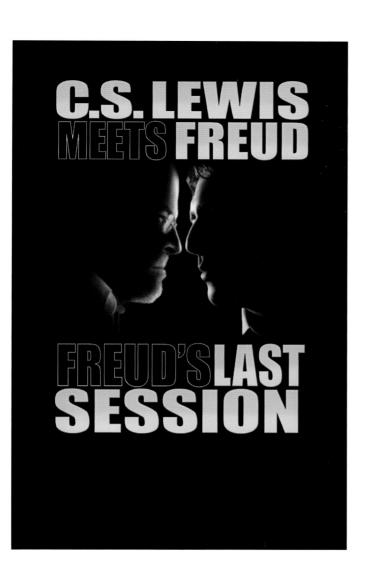

Freud's Last Session (2010)

This wonderful play by Mark St. Germaine was a surprise hit and drew crowds to a little known Upper West Side theatre. The simple construct is the meeting of Sigmund Freud and C. S. Lewis toward the end of Freud's life. Their confrontational conversations show men of very strong opinions debating on various topics with two differing points of view. Graphically, I saw it as sparring. I designed this piece to resemble prizefight posters that often use the format of the opponents standing nose-to-nose. Also, incorporating both names as the tag line helped highlight the show's two huge "star" selling points: Freud and C. S. Lewis.

The Belle of Amherst (2014)

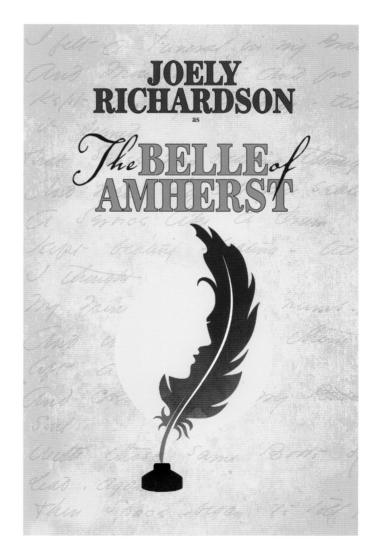

Actress Julie Harris certainly left an indelible mark on the role of Emily Dickinson. Not one to shy away from a challenge, the incandescent Joely Richardson brought this play back to Off-Broadway's Westside Theatre. It was a lovely production helmed by veteran producer Don Gregory. The goal here was to make this Victorian one-woman show look very contemporary while retaining its period essence. The quill pen certainly exemplifies the era, and using a graphic treatment rather than a detailed, illustrative one, I feel it answered all criteria. The cameo-like profile and authentic ghosted Dickinson handwriting added a genuine tone.

Making Movies (1990)

This Aaron Sorkin comedy concerned itself with a film director making a movie about Marines in Guam. Unfortunately, the film was being shot on location in Schenectady. I wanted to give the artwork a wry sense of irony. I thought the smiling director's chair perfectly captured the tone of the piece. It played at the long-lost Promenade Theatre where window cards of past shows lined the walls of the lobby and the staircases leading up to the seating area. It was always one of my favorite houses, and I got to revisit the posters I designed for many of the plays and musicals that opened there.

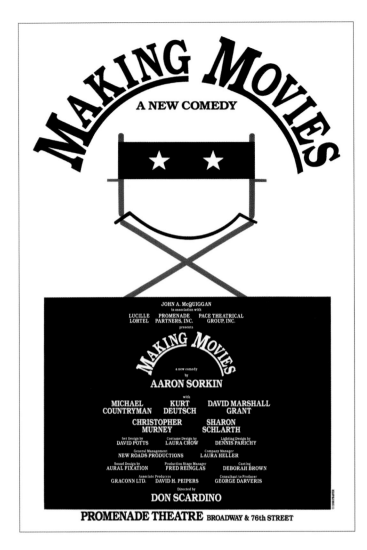

The Kathy and Mo Show (1989

What fun it was working with the brilliant writers and performers Kathy Najimy and Mo Gaffney. Ellen Krass produced what was to become one of Off-Broadway's biggest hits of 1989. Immortalized as an HBO special, the show is a compilation of vignettes that celebrates women. One of my favorite memories of working on this project was having game night at our apartment with Kathy when she and I realized we were huge board game-playing fanatics!

When I was asked to design key artwork for this marvelous musical, it had already gained a stellar reputation playing venues across the country. Those wacky princesses moved into NYC's St. Clement's Theatre where the show quickly caught fire and sold out every performance. After that run, it moved to the Westside Theatre (one of my favorites), allowing even more audiences to experience and enjoy this magical musical comedy, which features some of the funniest women in town! It was a great pleasure getting to meet and work with the creators, Dennis Diacino and Fiely Matias. I explored many concepts before hitting on the darts-in-the-apple idea. But as soon as the creative group saw it, they knew it fit the bill!

Himself and Nora (2016)

I am an avid reader, however, I have always been hesitant about tackling James Joyce's massive classic *Ulysses*. Since this new musical by Jonathan Brielle concerned itself with Joyce's steamy relationship with his future wife, Nora, I decided to take the plunge and open the novel after reading the script. It helped supply extra added inspiration during my graphic exploration. The play is an extraordinary account of the near-pornographic correspondence the couple shared through a series of letters written over the years. Since it was often rumored that Joyce literally wrote down Nora's words for use in his novel, I created this decidedly sensuous pen. Producer Cherie King loved it instantly.

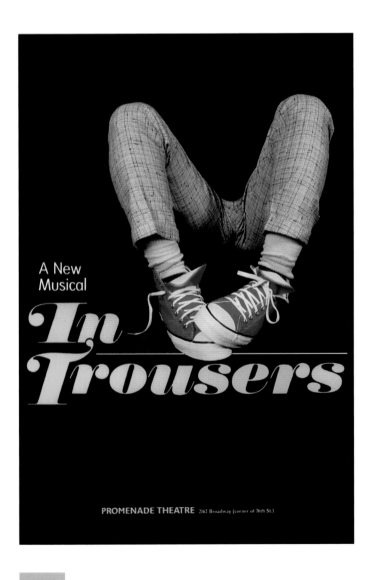

In Trousers (1985)

Continuing his *March of the Falsettos* story, William Finn's main character, Marvin, tells us about his previous loves and crushes that lead up to the realization that he's gay. I wanted to have an image that was quirky, sexy, and unexpected: a photo of a young man's legs that create a heart shape. The actual legs belonged to an assistant in our office who also happened to be the male pair of legs in my *Sunday in the Park with George* poster.

Photography by John Reilly

A Stage Version By
DEREK WALCOTT

THE ODYSSEY

Theatre at St. Clement's
423 West 46th Street

The Odyssey (2002)

I was told that this production was going to tell the classic story in a non-traditional way. So thinking outside of the box was in order. I really liked the idea of modern traffic signs in the middle of the Mediterranean as a way of warning our hero of his upcoming dangers and obstacles. Producer/ General Manager Roger Gindi also allowed me to have some fun designing the front of house. I believe he still has some of the street signs hanging in his office.

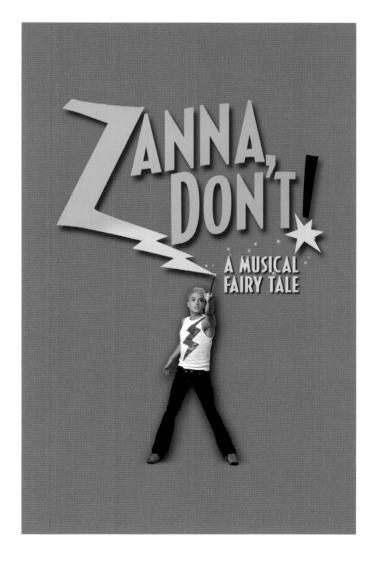

Zanna, Don't! (2003)

This unassuming little show caused quite a stir, garnered rave reviews and a Drama Desk nomination for Outstanding Musical due to its originality, great young cast, and terrific score. It takes place in a fairy-tale America where the majority of the world is gay, with heterosexuals subject to heterophobia. The story is told within a high school year. Producer Jack Dalgleish asked me to design a logo that would stand alone as artwork. I approached it from the viewpoint of something I might've scrawled on one of my high school notebooks, only with cleaner edges and brighter colors. The original printed window cards had glitter applied to them in a spot varnish. The poster shown here was the version designed to accommodate a photograph of star Jai Rodriguez, pre-*Queer Eye*, as Zanna.

Photography by Joan Marcus

Endpapers (2002)

Working out where to place each character in relation to the oversized books was a bit like assembling a jigsaw puzzle. A fair amount of Photoshop manipulation was involved post shoot, but that was an expected part of the design challenge.

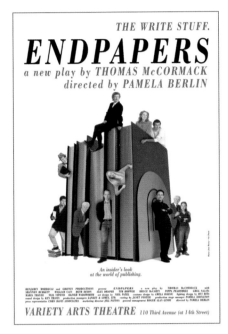

Photography by Joan Marcus

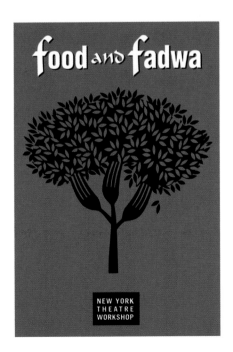

Tapestry (1993)

Years before the recent Broadway musical *Beautiful*, there was this tribute to Carole King at the Union Square Theatre. The very bold, graphic music note always made the art a standout in newspaper ads.

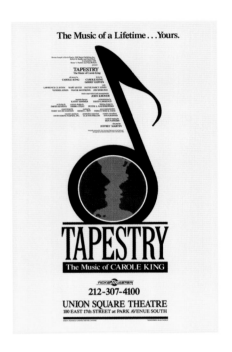

Food and Fadwa (2012)

I created this graphic to cull the elements of domesticity, cuisine, and family in one simple, fun image, keeping the tone on the lighter side for this charming play.

Out of the Mouths of Babes (2016)

A bevy of first-rate theatre actresses were fun to watch in this Israel Horovitz play about four women who arrive at the Paris apartment they had shared, at different times, with the same man, now deceased. The place is filled with artwork, including a Picasso. That led me to create the cubist women, and a cat, inspired by his work. My original poster design was deemed too serious, but the notion was correct. So, I lightened and brightened the style, maintaining the cubist flavor, to match the tone of this entertaining comedy.

Shakespeare's R&J (1998)

A rethinking of *Romeo & Juliet*, this riveting production relied on nothing but incredible acting and the words of William Shakespeare. It played in a small black box space with a cast of four actors wearing street clothes and portraying all the roles. *R&J* featured two of my favorite stage actors, Sean Dugan and Danny Gurwin. I originally designed the torn notebook-page logo as the only artwork, but later expanded on it with an illustration run through my office copier countless times, which gave it a no-frills look. The show received across-the-board rave reviews and ran for about a year.

CHAPTER FIVE
BEYOND

In organizing this poster book, it was necessary to sectionalize my work. What about the regional show posters? The institutional theatre posters? The international posters? The other New York City production posters that did not fall into the Broadway or Off-Broadway categories? This part of the book will feature those, aiming a special spotlight on the organizations and personalities that allowed me the opportunity to contribute visuals to their theatrical projects.

Over the years, I've come to resign myself to the fact that many theatre productions do not print window cards at all. As a poster enthusiast, I bemoan that recent trend. Online advertising has, in some instances, outdated having to actually use posters to advertise a play or musical. I think fondly of the days when the ad agency would hire guys to prowl the city in the dead of night to paste up wild postings on construction sites to announce a new show. Buying an e-mail blast is more affordable than printing a few hundred window cards, although the window cards will last forever.

During his last years producing, I worked on many shows with the great impresario Alexander H. Cohen. He was a charmer with a wicked sense of humor. One of his quirks was that he never wanted to print window cards of his shows until after opening night. The reason? "I don't want the wall of Joe Allen's restaurant to be filled with posters from my productions!" he'd always explain. "We'll wait for the reviews first!" For those who aren't familiar with the reference, Joe Allen is a famed theatrical hangout known for having its restaurant walls lined with framed posters from short-lived shows. I have quite a few on exhibit.

That's one of my favorite elements about what I do for a living. The poster design image is the first thing anyone sees about a show, be it Broadway, Off-Broadway, regional, or beyond! And, after the production has run its course, for better or for worse, the poster is the one thing that remains. It's a tangible, two-dimensional memory of a live event you'll never forget.

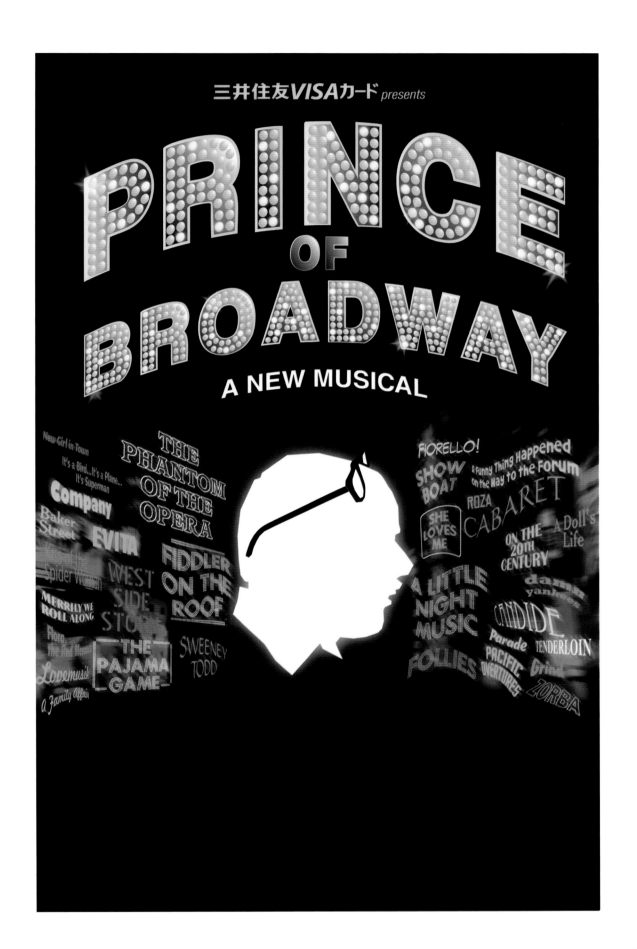

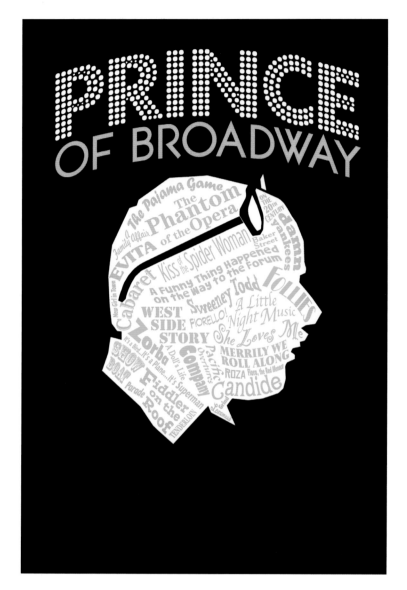

I believe I was asked to design the art for *Prince of Broadway* because I've had a long history of working on Harold Prince's shows, having created posters for *Sweeney Todd*, *Candide* at Lincoln Center, and *A Doll's Life*. This production was to premiere in Tokyo presented by Umeda Arts Theatre. I met with the producers in New York City and, via interpreter, we had a great conversation about Mr. Prince and his massive artistic contribution to Broadway. Then, I went to work. Needless to say, there was a wealth of show pictures to use as inspiration. But, to me, the image that instantly came to mind was Mr. Prince with his eyeglasses up and resting on his forehead (his most singular look)—very simple and graphic, à la *The Lion King*. I presented many posters, but the producers were immediately drawn to the simplicity of the design of the graphic Prince profile. I had also designed a version of the graphic profile that housed all of the show titles connected with Mr. Prince in his career. After a few weeks, the producers, now back home in Japan, corresponded via e-mail and asked for revisions. They wanted to remove the show titles from the art and see a revised title treatment with more realistic lights. After that step, a few weeks later, they asked that I design the show titles back into the art with the "feeling" of Broadway/Times Square. That was the final image used. And, although I like its dynamic impact, I still prefer my original concept.

Photography by Sherri Cohen

Jekyll & Hyde (1990)

A full seven years before it eventually opened on Broadway, I designed the first poster for Frank Wildhorn's most popular musical. I presented more than fifty pieces of art before Mr. Wildhorn and sponsor AT&T settled on the high contrast image. It was used to great effect on the double CD featuring the Jekyll art on disc 1 and the Hyde art on disc 2. My co-worker Dante Mele was kind enough to pose as both personas for the terrific photographer Sherri Cohen. Representatives from the ad agency and I attended the premiere production at the Alley Theatre in Houston, Texas. After the performance, we sauntered over to the gala opening night party. As soon as I entered, folks were coming up to me saying things like, "Congratulations!" and "Great job!" I wondered how any of them knew I'd designed the poster. Not more than fifteen minutes into this newfound fame, I realized everyone was confusing me for *Jekyll & Hyde*'s leading man, Chuck Wagner!

Agatha Christie's The Mousetrap (London, 1990)

This murder mystery had been playing in London since 1952. At long last, an American producer had gotten the rights for the U.S. It was to open out of town with an all-star cast. I created this logo, which was approved and ready to go. Something went completely awry and the entire production disintegrated. I was very fond of the poster and was disappointed it would never be seen. Fast forward to 2002. I'm in London and decide to finally see *The Mousetrap*, then celebrating its fiftieth anniversary! At the theatre I sauntered over to the souvenir nook where, lo and behold, there was my fingerprint-mouse logo on sweatshirts, key rings, and in the program! I was both elated and angry. I did confront the American producer upon my return to NYC, but still loved wearing my *Mousetrap* sweatshirt in London's St. Martin's Theatre, where the air-conditioning was set to sub-zero temperatures!

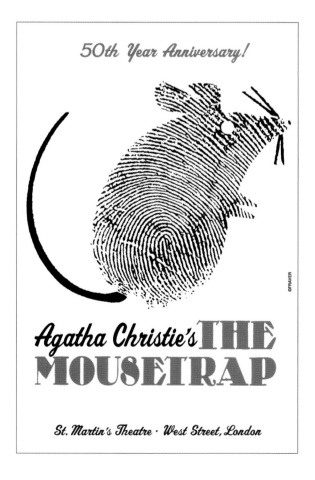

Appropriate (2016)

This play by the MacArthur Genius Grant Recipient Branden Jacobs-Jenkins packs a powerful punch. My thought here was a shadow box filled with family memories, some disturbing and mysterious. The window device was ideal to frame disparate images, and to give the feeling of peering in on someone else's private affairs. This was my first season designing for Westport Country Playhouse and working with Mark Lamos, Annie Keefe, and Peter Chenot. This Connecticut theatre is so rich in history. The lobby walls are covered in window cards from seasons long ago when the likes of Eva Le Gallienne, Tallulah Bankhead, and John Barrymore trod the boards. Its bold artistic vision and a facility steeped in theatrical history make it well worth a visit!

WESTPORT COUNTRY PLAYHOUSE

The Italian Girl in Algiers (2012)

I have to admit, I was not at all familiar with this Rossini masterpiece. Its libretto is filled with humor and the music is glorious. I wanted this piece to be as alluring as the titular character who captures the eye of the Turkish Bey. This poster eventually went through a number of minor revisions, but here you see the original the way it was first presented.

JACK VIERTEL & ROB BERMAN
ENCORES! ARTISTIC DIRECTOR & ENCORES! MUSIC DIRECTOR

The first time Fraver walked into the conference room at City Center, with rough poster art ideas locked in the iPad in his hand, we knew that Broadway history was colliding with Broadway history in a great way.

Fraver—we had no idea he had another name—had created the iconic images by which scores of Broadway shows were identified and first introduced, long before there was even a first preview. These included Stephen Sondheim and Hal Prince's *Sweeney Todd*. Now he was here to show us imagery for our presentation of Sondheim and Prince's *Merrily We Roll Along*. There was something poetic about the whole situation.

At Encores!, we are busy keeping Broadway's past alive in the present, and Frank Verlizzo (that turned out to be his name) is a key part of making the history we celebrate, and showing it to audiences even before they encounter the show itself. We ourselves have often gotten our first look at what to expect from a new musical from Fraver's artwork and the messages it sends.

As Encores! has grown up over the last twenty-five years, we have re-discovered again and again the various ways of sending our message visually, so it was only appropriate that Frank had studied with David Byrd, who had done Encores! poster art in the preceding years.

In that first meeting, Frank opened up his iPad and began to flip through image after image that presented visual statements of what we strive to achieve: romance, musicality, wit, charm, and drama. His images tell stories, or imply what's behind them, or both. And they are a pleasure to look at. Each one (he does three or four for each show) is informed by something in the piece that touches him. Almost as impressive as the artwork itself is that he offers four options that are each very different and represent contrasting approaches. It actually causes us to think and rethink what we want to emphasize within our productions.

Visually and conceptually he is remarkably prolific. He reads the scripts of the shows, watches whatever footage is available from previous productions, and thinks long and hard about thematic content, as well as setting, feeling, and characters. His work is an art like any other aspect of theatre-making. Each image he presents, it could be argued, is the right one. The one thing that is immediately clear is that Fraver is the right one.

What follows that "first look" is always among the most pleasurable discussions of the season, and the agony of having to choose. Among our favorites have been *Paint Your Wagon* with the gold heat of the sun pervading the background and the great character in the faces of the hardscrabble father and longing daughter. The wit of the comic book image for *Superman* made us incredibly happy, and the little cluster of New York socialites crowded in the "O" of *The New Yorkers,* perfectly captured the essence of that show's sophisticated cartoon world. Admittedly, the agony of choosing one image for each show is a sweet kind of agony. But, like most musicals (*Sweeney Todd* is a notable exception, of course), it can be counted upon to have a happy ending. Which only goes to show that Fraver is Fraver, no matter what his real name may be.

City Center was about to unveil the spectacular renovation of its theatre. To give their graphics a fresh start a new format had been created to house all of their posters and ads. This presented a particular challenge for me. After a career of designing posters in a vertical format (14" × 22"), the new City Center look left me with an extremely horizontal space in which to design, since the required billing for each show would live on the bottom third of the poster. After I recovered from the shock, I found it a refreshing design exercise. It may not sound very complex to you, but I found it difficult to think horizontally after more than thirty years of designing vertically!

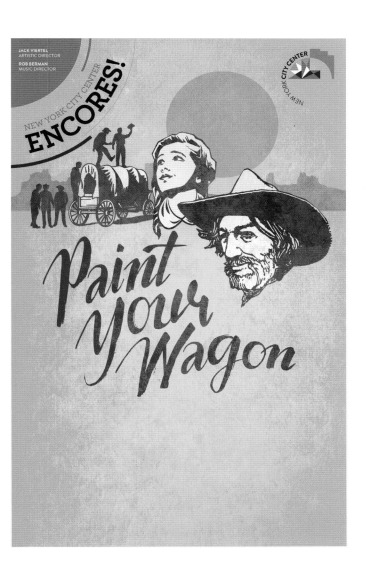

Paint Your Wagon (2015)

This is a rarely performed musical with a glorious Lerner and Loewe score. After presenting my original designs, an earlier version of this poster was chosen by Jack Viertel and Rob Berman, which prominently featured the young Jennifer character. I was asked to play her image down and bring to the forefront the prospector Ben, who is Jennifer's father. When I work on Encores!, I am designing months in advance of any casting choices. I very much follow the lead of Jack and Rob in the types of actors they imagine will fill the roles. For Ben, they asked for "very, very grizzled" and for the girl "younger." Keith Carradine and Alexandra Socha look as if they posed for the artwork! They seem to perfectly fit the description I was given of their roles.

... It's Superman (2013)

A Lois Lane and Superman fan since childhood, it always made me smile to think that just by wearing eyeglasses, this handsome hunk could hoodwink a really sharp ace reporter into thinking he was two different men. That was my first thought when asked to design for this most entertaining musical whose full title is *It's a Bird . . . It's a Plane . . . It's Superman*. Playing around with the oversized graphic comic book dots was also great fun. Both Jack Viertel and Rob Berman reacted positively to this poster right away.

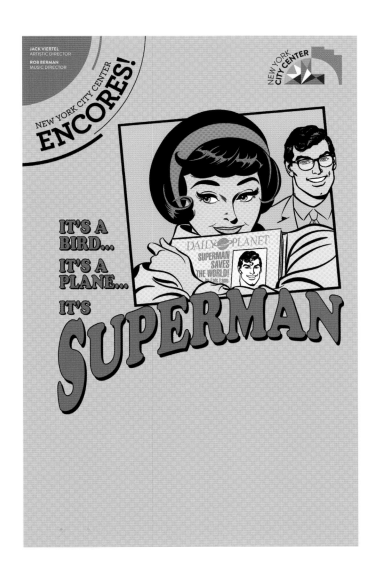

Cabin in the Sky (2016)

Originally produced in 1940, *Cabin in the Sky* followed *Porgy and Bess* in celebrating African-American music and dance traditions. Starring the glorious Norm Lewis, Chuck Cooper, and LaChanze, this lost treasure of a score includes the jazz hit "Taking a Chance on Love." Encores! restored the show to its original glory with a wonderful production. My goal here was to create a poster reminiscent of a big MGM dance musical.

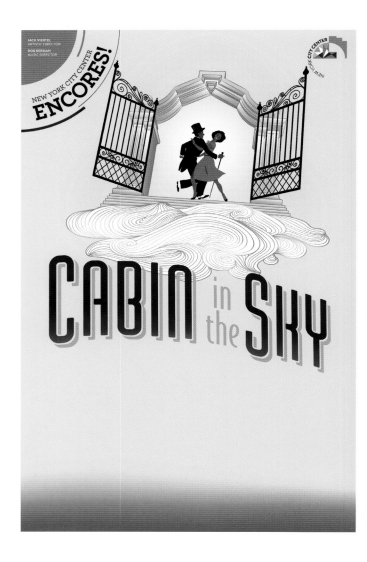

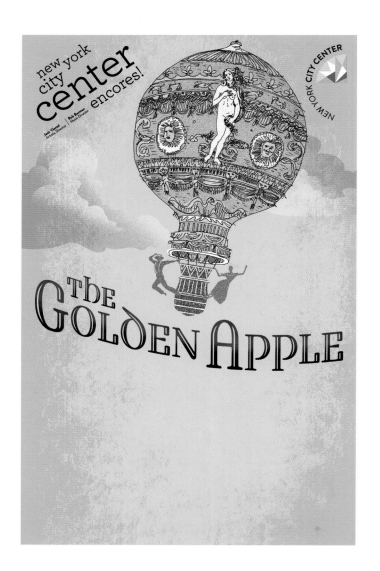

The Golden Apple (2017)

The mission of Encores! is to present rarely heard works of some of America's most important composers and lyricists. *The Golden Apple*, written by John Latouche, fit that bill perfectly, having accumulated a rabid cult following. It is a very ambitious musical based on *The Odyssey* but set in the American Northwest of the early twentieth century. The composer, Jerome Moross, studied under Aaron Copland and the lush score reflects that. It was an ambitious undertaking and was beautifully done!

It's always a major thrill for me when asked to design poster art for anything by Stephen Sondheim! Since the setting of the show is Venice, I wanted to convey a bit of the awe experienced by the main character, Leona, played by the exquisite Melissa Errico. I found a fitting focus in the floppy sun hat, which created a tourist-on-vacation symbol instantly. This is the only collaboration of musical theatre giants Richard Rodgers and Stephen Sondheim. Having talented musical theatre eye-candy Claybourne Elder on stage was also a plus!

Big River (2017)

Based on the classic Mark Twain novel, this musical definitely presents a design challenge. The book is sprawling in scope. It almost forces one to focus on the two main characters, Huck and Jim, and their rafting adventures on the Mississippi River. I experimented with a variety of graphic styles. This dreamy, storybook-type illustration was the winner.

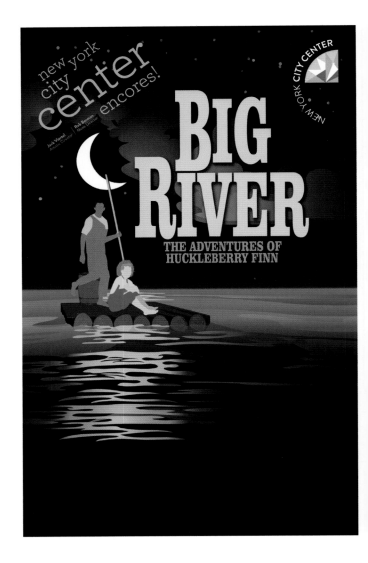

Zorba (2015)

I was particularly excited by this project because I'd never seen (nor heard the score from) this Kander and Ebb classic. It's a terrific story about the friendship between two very different men. There's drama, comedy, colorful village characters, and murder thrown into the musical mix. It takes place on the Greek island of Crete, so I wanted the art to recall the style of a vintage travel poster. On the technical side of things, I discovered a wonderful Photoshop technique that I employed to create the water. The great thing about technology is that it sometimes does allow time for me to experiment with various ways of approaching a challenge.

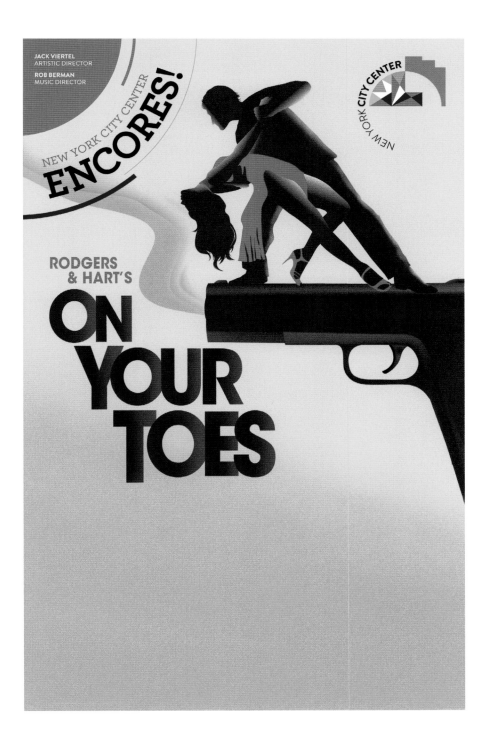

I had a vague recollection of having seen the 1984 revival production of this show. Historically, *On Your Toes* marked the first time a Broadway musical made dramatic use of classical dance and incorporated jazz into its score. Since the story takes place in the 1930s, I chose to do the art in the style of my favorite poster designer, A. M. Cassandre. The travel posters he created in the '30s are iconic. It was an honor to create an homage to an artist I admire for this wonderful Rodgers and Hart musical comedy.

Irma La Douce (2014)

This selection from 1960 certainly lives up to Encores! original mission to present little known and rarely produced musicals. My inspiration for this poster art came from the whimsical line illustrations one can find in French textbooks of the period. I sporadically attempt to learn French, hence I've collected quite a few vintage volumes. It's also noted in the script that Irma wears a lot of green. I have no idea if that was symbolic of something, but it helped guide my color palette. My goal was to capture the lighthearted nature of this musical.

Little Me (2014)

The buxom Belle Poitrine character usually takes second place when one thinks of *Little Me* since the musical typically showcases the talent of a single actor playing multiple roles as her husbands and beaus. In this terrific Encores! production, taking center stage was Tony Award-winner Christian Borle. In designing the poster art, however, I felt that it was time to give Belle, played by Judy Kaye and Rachel York, her due. The concept showing Belle actually juggling her many men gives the art a fun, lively quality that this breakneck musical certainly possesses in spades! I can only hope I did justice to the hysterical Neil Simon book and blockbuster score by Cy Coleman and Carolyn Leigh.

Pipe Dream (2011)

Written in 1955 by the legendary Rodgers and Hammerstein, this musical is rarely produced. What a perfect vehicle for Encores! *Pipe Dream* is based on the stories of John Steinbeck, which take place in Cannery Row, a fishing town. It's an oddball romantic comedy involving prostitutes and unemployed fishermen. After seeing quite a few of my designs, Jack Viertel and Rob Berman chose this very simple graphic illustration. Admittedly, after watching a performance months later, I realized that the poster was indeed a perfect representation of the show. I guess Ted Chapin did as well, since R&H acquired it for their licensing division.

The Most Happy Fella (2014)

Frank Loesser's romantic musical has an astonishing score. In doing research, I found that most of the past poster imagery for this show involved the main character, an aging Napa Valley farmer, skipping around grapevines. I was more inspired by colorful fruit crate labels and used that concept as my device to house the rather lengthy title, which now included the composer's name. The figures of the two main characters were taken from an alternate poster design I had presented. Both Jack Viertel and Rob Berman liked the figures and asked if they could be incorporated into my "label" poster art. A request to combine two different designs is sometimes a scary proposition but, in this case, I feel it actually enhanced the poster.

This madcap musical from the Roaring Twenties is the first hit collaboration from George and Ira Gershwin. It ushered in the Golden Age of American Musical Comedy. When first reading the script, I was a bit overwhelmed by the number of characters as well as the convoluted, zany plot line. In distilling all the varied pieces, I decided the important elements to convey were elegant period fun with lots of singing and dancing. The butler's gloved hand holding the gold tray certainly exemplifies the kind of stylish wealth that was often the setting for these flapper comedies.

Gentlemen Prefer Blondes (2011)

The original stage production starred Carol Channing, which was followed by a radically reimagined film version with Marilyn Monroe. The show takes place in 1924. Since Encores! was recreating the original score and orchestrations, I took my lead from the style of design most popular in the Roaring Twenties: art deco. The most famous song in the musical is "Diamonds Are a Girl's Best Friend," so I thought it would be fun to represent the madcap gold digger, Lorelei Lee, with a vintage caricature made of the gems.

The New Yorkers (2017)

Prohibition was never this entertaining! This 1930 Cole Porter musical celebrates gangsters, society dames, and bathtub gin and it was the surprise hit of the Encores! season. It is a madcap romp that takes the audience from Park Avenue to Sing-Sing and back again. Much of the original material had been lost, so this was Encores! most ambitious musical reconstruction to date. Tapping into the style of the period to create the artwork was a treat!

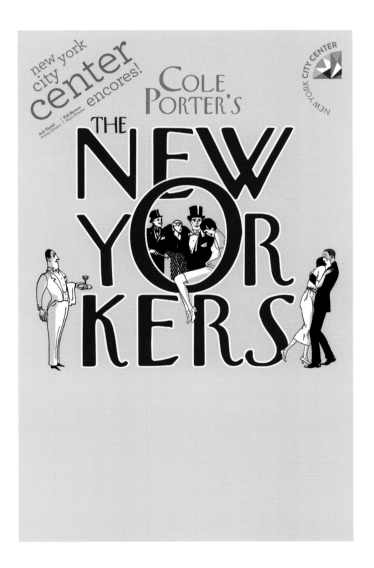

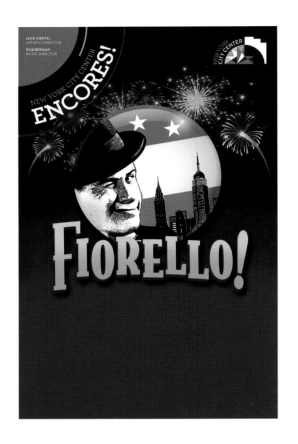

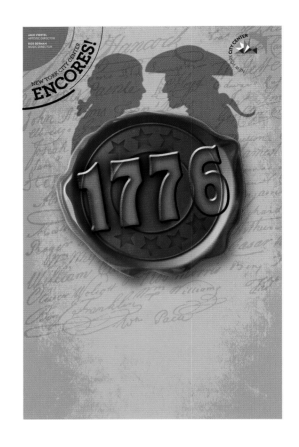

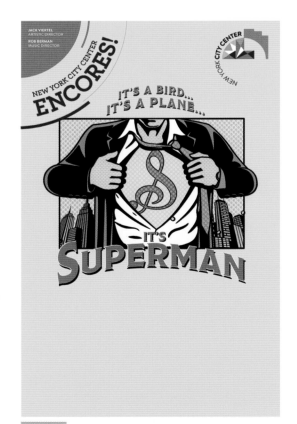

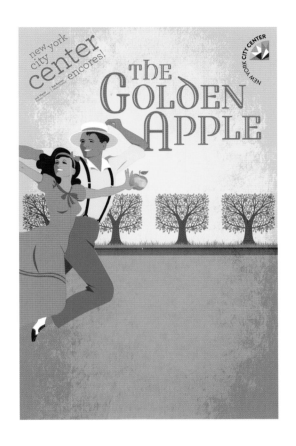

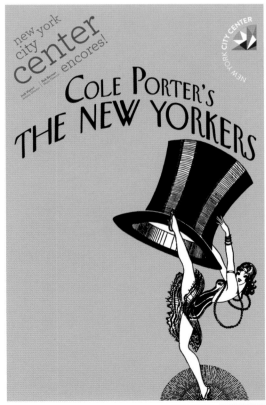

COMMENTARY

WILLIAM HAYES
PRODUCING ARTISTIC DIRECTOR OF PALM BEACH DRAMAWORKS

Theatre posters are marketing tools. Great theatre posters are also works of art. And Frank Verlizzo is a master artist. Fraver has been designing the show posters for Palm Beach Dramaworks (PBD) since the 2011–2012 season, and every eye-catching, evocative image brilliantly and creatively captures some essential quality about each play.

I can't overstate the importance of a theatre poster. You get just one chance to make a first impression, and in the theatre the first image the public sees is the poster. A successful poster doesn't just advertise a play, it makes a statement that piques the curiosity of the viewer—hopefully to the point of buying a ticket.

Some of the best posters, like some of the best works of art—be they paintings or plays—are a bit enigmatic; that is, they can convey different things to different people. And Fraver has a gift for finding the truth about a play, while at the same time trusting the imagination of the viewer to fill in the blanks.

Before he begins his designs, we have a brief preliminary conversation about the tone of each play. I don't give him ideas or suggest images; he reads the plays and responds as an artist. He will then present me with his posters, and we'll discuss each image. On occasion, he will modify an image based on my reaction. Sometimes a discussion isn't even necessary: I was immediately blown away by his illustration for *Exit the King*, in which he brilliantly encapsulated Ionesco's dark humor.

When I first approached Fraver about designing the show posters for Palm Beach Dramaworks, I was a little intimidated. He was perhaps the most successful poster artist on Broadway, and I had no idea how he would react to working with a regional theatre that had only recently begun to make a name for itself. I needn't have worried. He was not only gracious, but he believed in our mission and was eager to work with us. He is as fine a person as he is an artist, and I am thrilled that he is part of the Palm Beach Dramaworks family.

The Cripple of Inishmaan (2016)

This dark comedy links its plot line to the real life filming of a documentary made in Hollywood. This connection led me to a stark graphic image that is at once funny and troubling. I again employed my favorite color palette of red, black, and white.

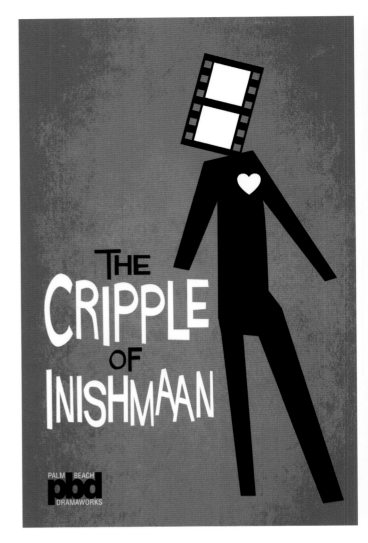

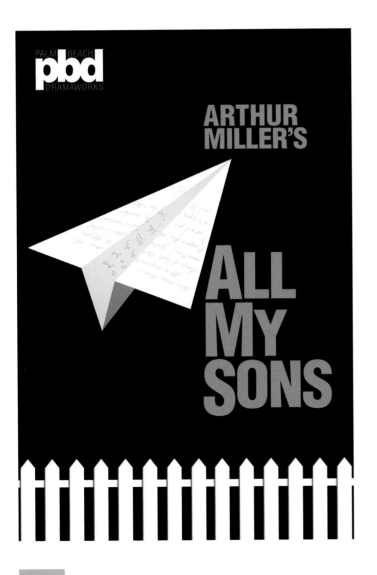

All My Sons (2011)

Palm Beach Dramaworks is a class act, now housed in their beautiful theatre on Clematis Street. The opening production, in the new theatre was this Arthur Miller classic. I purposely kept it simple, mixing a vintage feel with a contemporary graphic treatment. The thinking here was to capture a bit of Americana using the white picket fence and paper airplane, on which a pivotal plot note was written.

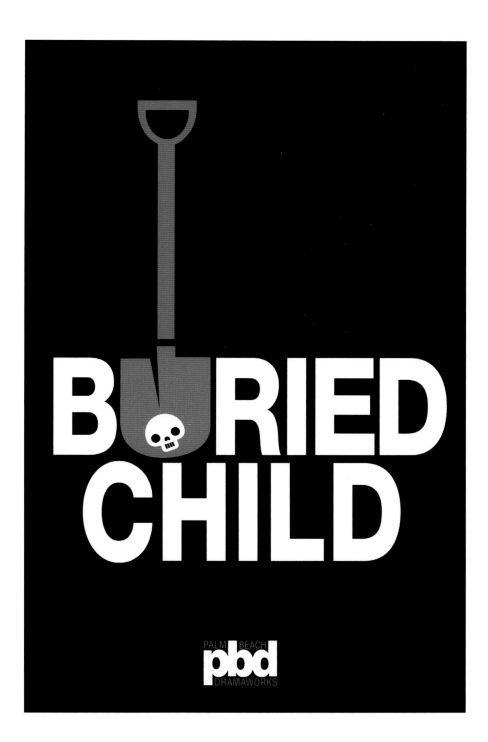

This Sam Shepard masterpiece is certainly a tough one—very dark, very oppressive, and highly theatrical. Both Dramaworks's heads Bill Hayes and Sue Ellen Beryl immediately reacted strongly to this stark graphic. The bold black, white, and red combination is always a major favorite of mine to employ.

Having seen numerous productions of this Eugene O'Neill masterpiece, I wanted to give the poster a timeless atmosphere, a sense of one day blurring into the next. With this moody illustration, I hoped to capture the tone of the play in a deceptively simple image.

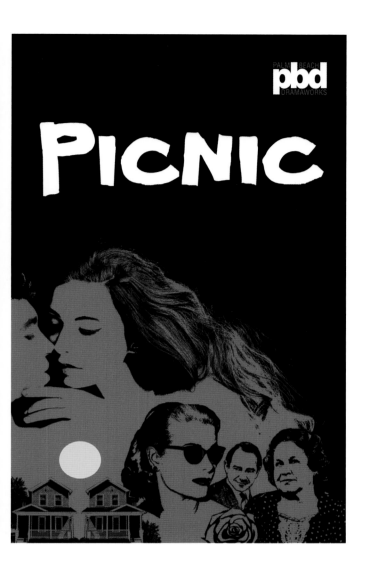

One of the delights of designing for PBD is that I get to create posters for plays I missed their first time around. *Picnic* first premiered on Broadway in 1953. For his production, director Bill Hayes asked me to incorporate the actors' likenesses in my illustration. Few plays are as smoldering with underlying sex as this William Inge masterpiece.

The Pitmen Painters (2011)

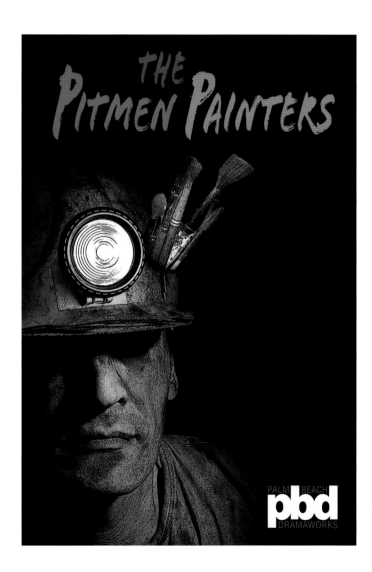

Lee Hall's extraordinary play takes place in 1930s England. It concerns the true story of the Ashington Group, a faction of miners who hire a tutor from their local school to teach them the art of painting. I created the dark image of the miner as juxtaposition to the artistic expression they seek. I felt this represented the arguments so beautifully expressed in the play, and made for an arresting image as well.

A Raisin in the Sun (2012)

Lorraine Hansberry's enduring play demonstrates the power of having a dream. In this instance, the dream of owning a house that would unite the Younger family. Nurturing a plant, standing up to bigotry, and determining to live a better life are all dramatic ingredients in this marvelous work. I wanted this poster to convey a strong feeling of hope.

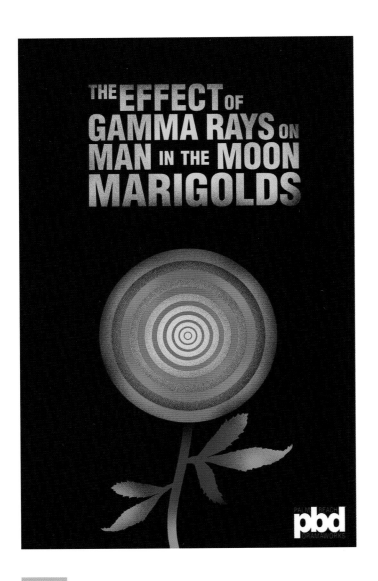

The Effect of Gamma Rays on Man-in-the-Moon Marigolds (2011)

This Pulitzer Prize-winner is rarely produced. The play revolves around a dysfunctional family consisting of a single mother and her two daughters, who try to cope with their abysmal status in life. The play is a lyrical drama, reminiscent of Tennessee Williams' style. I experimented here in Photoshop with the airbrush tool as well as with some special effects. My concept was to create a graphic that would grab your attention yet make you feel a bit uneasy. It was the way I reacted when reading this hypnotic masterwork.

I was thrilled to design for this Edward Albee drama. It has long been a favorite of mine. I wanted to keep the image very simple, yet uncomfortably bold. In the martini-soaked atmosphere of the play, I found this symbol struck just the right cord.

My Old Lady (2012)

It was big news that Estelle Parsons was coming to PBD to star in this Israel Horovitz play. Although her character in the show, Mathilde, is around ninety-four years old, I chose to illustrate her much younger, as in her unfolding back story. The setting is Paris and I chose to reveal that fact in the poster art. Who doesn't love Paris?

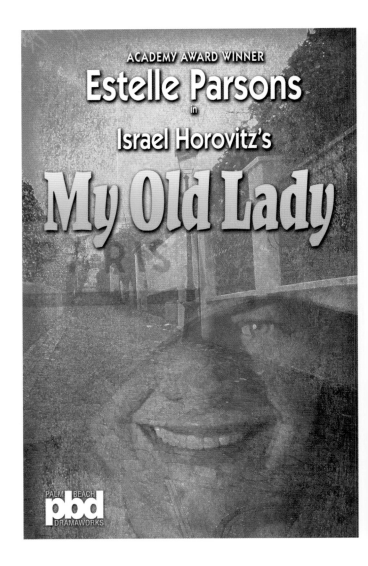

Tryst (2014)

This psychological thriller by Karoline Leach centers on a handsome con man who courts and marries vulnerable women until he may finally have met his match. Dramaworks requested an image that did not give away too many plot twists. After several conversations and quite a few tries, I very much like this solution. It looks dangerous, seductive, and disturbing.

Clearly, I never get tired of designing posters for this Tennessee Williams's play. This time around, I chose to focus on the struggle the Reverend Shannon must endure contending with the three strong-willed women in his life.

It began in Australia as an educational presentation but is now being reworked as a theatrical piece. *Dinosaur Zoo* still retains educational overtones about the Earth's history with a strong "be good to the Earth" message. Watch the excited faces of audiences on YouTube and you'll begin to understand the magic behind *Dinosaur Zoo*. These life-sized creations are a wonder to behold and you can quickly forget that they're puppets being manipulated right before your eyes. I was asked to design a fun, colorful logo that captured the nature of the performance. Since each dinosaur is created in exhaustively researched detail, it was important that my artwork be true to the aesthetic of the show's production company, Erth Visual & Physical, Inc. The other goal was not to make the art appear threatening in any way since their young audiences are looking more for adventure rather than being frightened out of their wits!

Eugene Onegin (2012)

I remember my mom taking me to the old Metropolitan Opera House on Broadway and 39th Street years before it fell victim to the wrecking ball. She was an avid Verdi lover and attended whenever she could. I saw *Madama Butterfly* with her there. It's a warm memory and instilled in me that theatre could be as grand as movies, only more tangible, and in person! Collecting motion picture soundtracks was a passion of mine from an early age, so hearing this lush orchestra live really impressed me. Fast forward almost fifty years and, naturally, I was duly excited when contacted by Portland Opera to tackle two of their upcoming productions. I know the opera world's schedule works even farther out than traditional theatre productions. It came as little surprise when I was asked to revise my already-approved piece for *Eugene Onegin* some months later. The marketing department had just learned that the director was updating it. You see the original here.

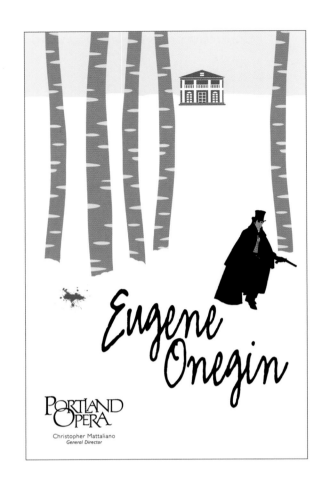

On the 20th Century (2005)

The Actors Fund was planning one of their gala concert events of this Comden-Green-Coleman-Prince musical, which is one of my favorite shows of all time. So I threw myself into this project with quite a lot of excitement. It is always challenging for me to design for a show that has already had an iconic piece of art created for its original production. Nicolas Gaetano had designed the most luscious art deco poster using the main characters about to board the train. I finally opted to concentrate on the Twentieth Century itself. I did a good deal of (fun) research, the results of which you see here in all its glory.

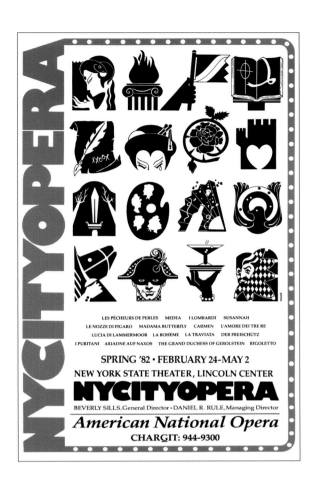

NYCityOpera (1982)

Beverly Sills was interested in creating a new look for her company. She reacted positively to these bold graphic images. They worked well on a page together and were equally effective when isolated and presented individually in advertising. I had many a pleasurable art meeting with the charming opera superstar. A radiant presence in her office, Ms. Sills was always dressed in the same elaborately bejeweled floor-length kaftan. I often wondered why that was. Decades later, and much older now, I finally have come to understand it. When something is comfortable and looks good on you, why not wear it all the time?

Theatre Museum (1979)

The Museum of the City of New York was renting space in midtown for their theatre collection and asked me to design a poster to commemorate the event. My thoughts immediately went to my mom, Nancy. As a grade school student, I can recall the countless trips we made to the Metropolitan Museum. I acquired my love for art, books, and museums from her. I drew a graphic version of her beautiful face and surrounded her with art deco trappings, a style of design I came to love studying under David Byrd. On this piece, I even gave Byrd a further nod by having my signature appear twice on the poster, something he often did. Unfortunately, the Theatre Museum was not a success, and there are very few of these posters to be found.

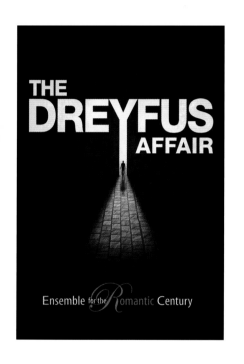

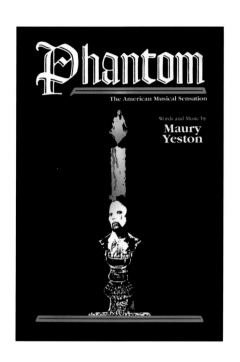

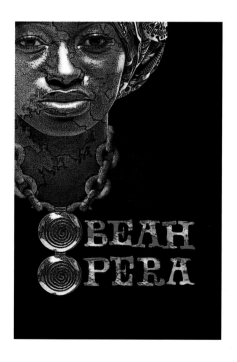

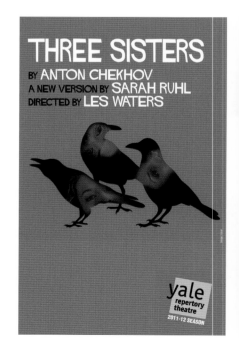

The Dreyfus Affair (2017)

TOP LEFT

Ensemble for the Romantic Century's work is a hybrid of classical music and live theatre. This show concerns itself with false arrest and intrigue. It's based on a true story of political passions and unswerving loyalty that resonates to this very day. I wanted the artwork to reflect the tension and suspense of the taut situation. It was staged at the Brooklyn Academy of Music (BAM) and starred my talented friend Max von Essen.

Phantom (1991)

TOP CENTER

Maurey Yeston's score for the musical *Nine* is one of my all-time favorites. I was elated when he asked that I work on artwork for his musical adaptation of *Phantom of the Opera*. Unfortunately, due to bad timing, Mr. Yeston was forced to postpone his version of the classic Gaston Leroux novel. When a story is this grand and operatic, the simpler the image, the more effective it is. I created an ornate candlestick using the heroine as the flame (a concept I carried over from one of my rejected *Carrie* posters presented for the original Broadway production). It was a visual device that pointed straight up to the bold, period title design. I am happy to report Mr. Yeston's *Phantom* has ultimately received more than 1,000 productions around the world!

These Paper Bullets! (2014)

TOP RIGHT

Mix a Shakespeare play, Carnaby Street of the swinging '60s, the music of Green Day's Billie Joe Armstrong, and you get this modish homage centering on a wildly popular rock band (think Beatles). The iconic imagery associated with the Fab Four is bountiful. I chose to take inspiration from the title design of their second film, *Help!*, for my logo. In doing research, I was struck by how many publicity photos of the four musicians show them jumping in the air. My silhouette drawing captures the feeling of those press pictures without infringing on any copyrights. Framing the whole thing as the cover of a 45 RPM record made it a cohesive unit.

Obeah Opera (2015)

BOTTOM LEFT

Created by the fabulous Nicole Brooks, this is a retelling of the legendary Salem witch trials from the perspective of Caribbean slave women. Sung entirely a cappella by an all-female cast, *Obeah Opera* is a dramatic work that gives the traditional opera form a shake-up. It draws from an array of different musical genres: spiritual, gospel, jazz, blues, Caribbean folk, traditional African, calypso, R&B, and reggae. It incorporates a variety of storytelling elements from the performing arts that includes musical theatre, opera, and dance. My aim was to give this piece the vibrant, worldly aura that it delivers.

The Visit (2013)

BOTTOM CENTER

The marketing guru at Yale Repertory Theatre asked if I'd try my hand at working with student directors to develop posters for their upcoming show projects. Director Cole Lewis chose *The Visit* for her Yale School of Drama presentation. This was the original 1956 play by Friedrich Dürrenmatt, not the Kander and Ebb musical adaptation. It is a dark, haunting, weirdly comedic piece about love, revenge, and murder. The leading lady's prosthetic ivory hand particularly intrigued me, and since the director agreed, it became the focus of the compelling artwork.

Three Sisters (2011)

BOTTOM RIGHT

This was the first poster I designed for Yale Repertory Theatre. I wanted to give this new version of the Chekhov classic, by the distinguished playwright Sarah Ruhl, a startlingly fresh graphic look. I also thought it important that Yale Rep start introducing bold color into its signage. Among all the muted browns (the university buildings), the greens (in spring), and snow whites (in winter), a bright color palette was definitely in order! I presented a variety of designs but the protective crows were a clear favorite.

DEAN PITCHFORD
SONGWRITER, SCREENWRITER, DIRECTOR, ACTOR, AND NOVELIST

One of the greatest (of many) challenges that any playwright or stage composer grapples with is how to open a show. The houselights dim, the curtain rises . . . and then what? When (if!) we creators finally get it right, that first page of dialogue or that first song contains within it the promise—in tone and style and content and craft—of everything that will follow.

Which, to me, makes Frank Verlizzo's work all the more astonishing. Think about it: he manages to capture and contain—in one, indelible image—the soul of a show. Before you read the reviews or buy your ticket or open your *Playbill,* Frank's poster has supplied a potent whiff of the experience that awaits you. He has to "start" the show before the show can even start.

As a longtime fan of Fraver, I was thrilled when I heard from the Rodgers & Hammerstein Organization that they had hired him to create new artwork for *Footloose.* The timing was fortuitous: my collaborators, Tom Snow and Walter Bobbie, and I had continued to work on the show after its Broadway run had ended in 2000, and we were just about to combine our revisions into a new edition of the show that the folks at R&H were referring to—internally—as *Footloose 2.0.* To conform the new rental materials with the Broadway cast recording, we dropped two songs from the original disc, recorded and inserted a song that had been cut out of town, and remastered the entire CD. What a perfect time to put a new "face" on the show, eh?

I requested a meeting with Frank before he began his work, and he readily agreed. He suggested that, before we go for drinks, we meet at the New York Public Library of Performing Arts at Lincoln Center, where a retrospective of his work was on view. Imagine walking through that jaw-dropping exhibition at the side of the show's artist! I still get chills.

Then, over drinks, I told him about the evolution of *Footloose,* starting with my writing the screenplay for the original motion picture in 1984. He expressed a deep affection for the film, an affection that eventually found its way into his artwork in the bright yellow of the title (a nod to the color of Kevin Bacon's Volkwagen in the movie) and the large windowpanes— which evokes the backdrop of warehouse windows against which Kevin's character, Ren, was filmed doing his "angry" dance.

And because a small town minister, Ren's adversary in the plot, figures so prominently in the story, I was tickled to spy a church steeple in the distance, placed in the exact center of the background.

Because the show is about a rambunctious Chicago native who finds himself in a small Midwest town where dancing is illegal, posters for the show from all over the world have often depicted our protagonist leaping, spinning, kicking, or sliding across a floor. In what I consider the most inspired and unexpected twist in Frank's artwork, he avoided that cliché by depicting Ren solidly planted, lost in the ecstasy of an air-guitar solo. A kinetic hero, definitely in motion, but not in flight.

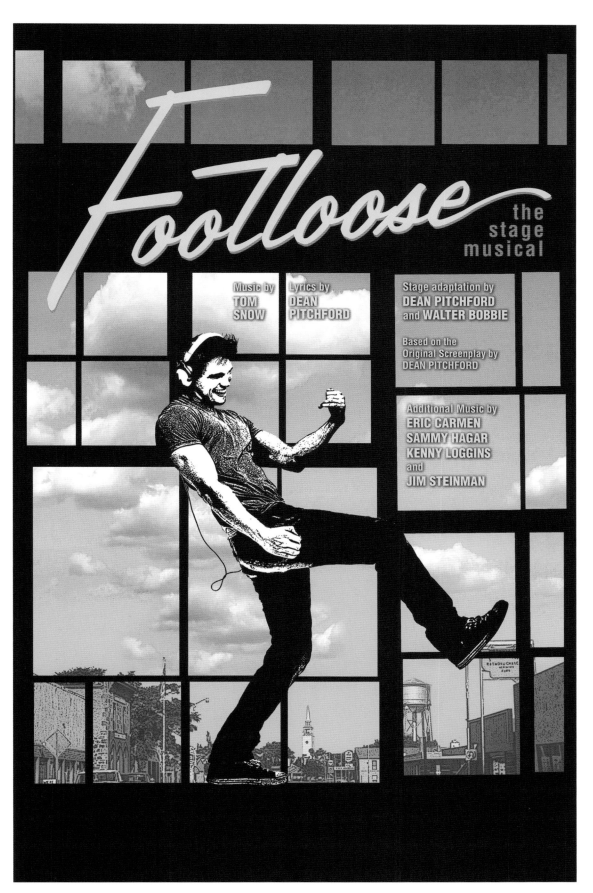

Courtesy of Rodgers & Hammerstein, an Imagem Company, www.rnh.com

COMMENTARY
DEAN PITCHFORD

The 2012 Off-Broadway revival of *Carrie*, which Michael Gore, Larry Cohen, and I had begun revising in 2009, gave new life to a show which had developed a rabid cult following around the world, despite the fact that it was never recorded or seen after its short-lived Broadway debut in 1988.

What's fascinating about Stephen King's debut novel, and all the iterations of it ever since, beginning with Brian DePalma's landmark 1976 motion picture, is that people see different stories in the tale of a bullied, marginalized high school girl who ultimately gets revenge on her tormentors. Some see a dark and brooding psychological study; others, a horror romp ending with Carrie's nasty classmates getting their just desserts.

But that's understandable. Carrie, after all, lives between two worlds: the raucous, high-energy environment of the high school where she suffers daily abuse and the candlelit, suffocating atmosphere of the home she shares with her religious fanatic of a mother.

When Michael, Larry, and I spoke with Frank as he began his work on the key art, we were comforted to hear that: 1.) He had seen the revival; 2.) He had loved it; and 3.) He totally "got" the duality of Carrie's reality and, consequently, the duality inherent in our show—swinging, as it does, between songs and scenes full of youthful energy and the highly-theatrical, near-operatic material created for Carrie and her overzealous mother.

In what Frank would later tell me was a first for him, he presented his final poster electronically, during a conference call between me (in Los Angeles), Michael and Larry (in Westchester, New York), and him and Dana Siegel of the R&H office (in New York City). Mid-conversation, we all logged onto a secure website, where Frank, with as much flourish as can be mustered over the Internet, "unveiled" this image. And Michael, Larry, and I—though separated by thousands of miles—simultaneously gasped, "Wow!" In the *Carrie* poster, as in the *Footloose* artwork, Frank has put the show's protagonist front and center. But in this one he has depicted her in silhouette, a mysterious, faceless figure onto whom an onlooker can project their own impression. Note the tensed shoulders and the hands stretched into near-claws. The eeriness of this image is heightened by the long shadow she casts, lit from behind by flames that almost appear to be dancing.

But this sinister tableau is balanced by the vibrant color scheme—the eye-popping yellows and oranges and reds, which are seen not only below the title treatment (the word *CARRIE* as if graffitied onto a gym locker), but are also reflected, winking, and whirling, in the giddy mirror ball high atop the frame. This single image promises not only drama, intrigue, and energy. But also fun.

Precisely what we hope our show delivers.

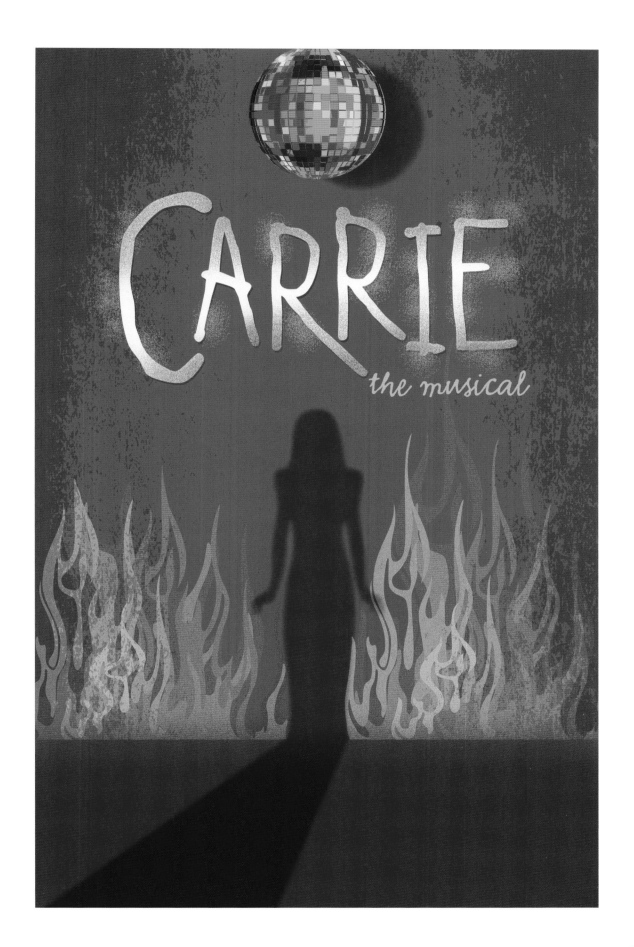

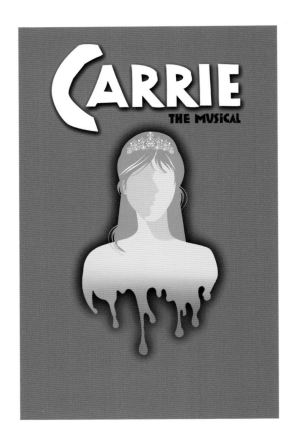

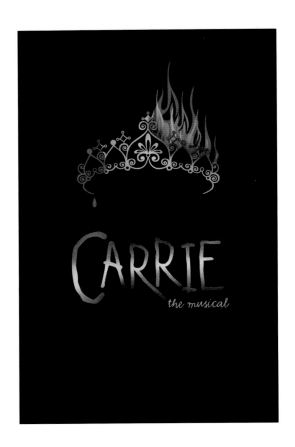

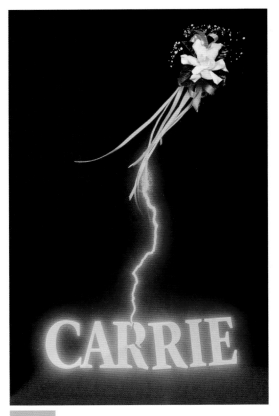

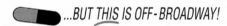

Valley of the Dolls (1996)

What lover of camp wouldn't be thrilled when asked to design the poster art for the Off-Broadway production that recreates the 1967 film and features Jackie Beat as Helen Lawson? I was especially proud of the copy line I'd written which parodied a famous quote from the movie: "Broadway doesn't go for booze and dope . . . but this is Off-Broadway!" The show was a wacky word-by-word recreation of the 20th Century Fox film. It received enthusiastic reviews but, unfortunately, we learned the producer hadn't secured the rights to the movie script (oops!) and it closed immediately.

Showstoppers! (2002)

Everyone fell in love with the singing diva! She was designed for this Gay Men's Health Crisis (GMHC) benefit concert. I played with basic shapes and drew her in a style reminiscent of '20s artist John Held. The poster certainly garnered a lot of attention for a one-night gig, and I received many requests for window cards. Unfortunately, none were ever printed.

Sex with Strangers (2016)

In designing my first season for Westport Country Playhouse, the artistic director, Mark Lamos, and I discussed the advantages of visually treating the artwork so that each show related to the others in the same graphic style. Ultimately, we decided it best to design each poster as an individual entity. I've worked it both ways when creating art for subscription-based organizations.

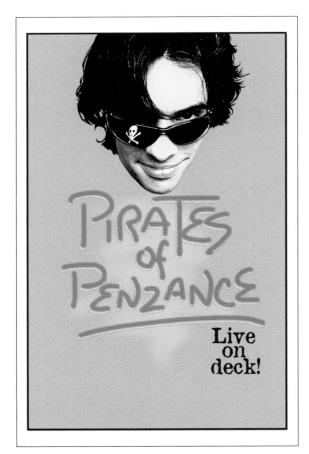

Pirates of Penzance (2000)

The unique take on this production was that it was staged in an alternative space: an actual three-masted ship docked at South Street Seaport. Needless to say, the budget was extremely tight. To give it a client-requested NYC-centric feel, I employed graffiti-style spray paint for the logo design. I thought the end result very fun and effective.

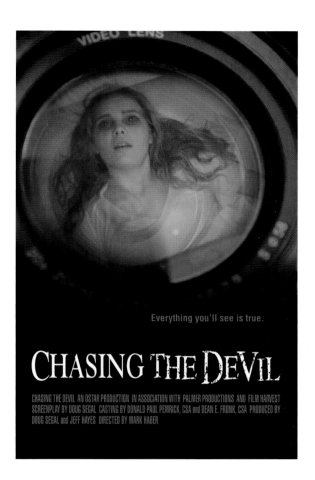

Chasing the Devil (2012)

A major fan of the horror genre, I was thrilled when Ostar and company asked me to come up with poster designs for their upcoming movie. For a short period during my stint at J. Walter Thompson Entertainment, I designed posters for a number of 20th Century Fox films. The process, at least in the early '80s, was unlike the "hands-on" family-feeling of creating poster art for Broadway. Each time I designed for a film, the presentation would be packed up and sent around the globe, in some cases to the various producers involved, who were now already working on other projects. Months would pass with no comment. Then, suddenly, everything would be sent back marked up with critiques and requested changes that had to be made immediately because of distributor deadlines. After a few projects like that, I decided theatre art was a much better fit for me. Of course, this was before the advent of technology. It was a much smoother and more pleasant process working on *Chasing the Devil* recently.

In a Year with 13 Moons (2012)

Rainer Werner Fassbinder shot part of his film, on which this play is based, in a meat-packing slaughterhouse. I wanted to retain the creepy feeling of menace he captured. By heightening and saturating the tones of contrasting colors purple and yellow, the poster image achieved a disturbing, eye-catching dread.

Photography by Joan Marcus

Waterfall (2015)

Set in 1933 Bangkok and Tokyo, a young Thai student falls in love with the American wife of a Thai diplomat. The story of their forbidden love has a gloriously romantic score written by the dynamic Maltby and Shire. This epic saga began its life at the Pasadena Playhouse. This promises to be a very exciting, original new musical—one with a real waterfall on stage!

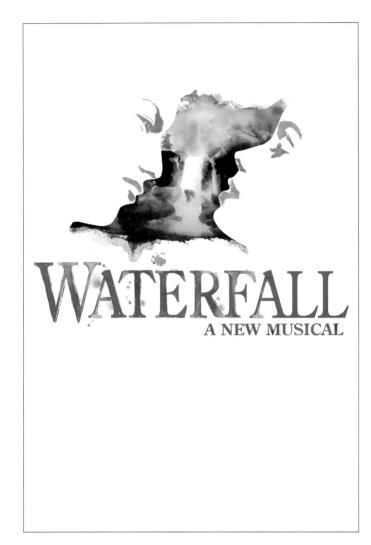

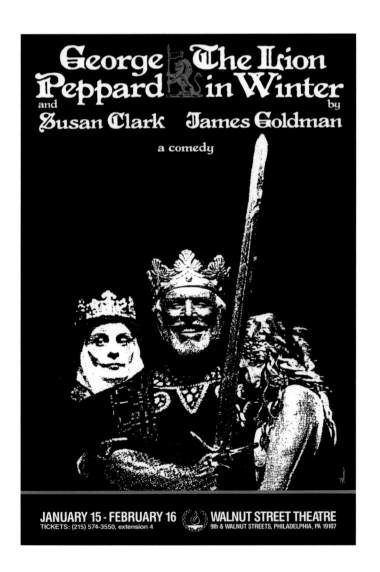

The Lion in Winter (1992)

I had long admired James Goldman's comedy-drama about King Henry II's family feud over his crown. But, enough about that. Let me tell you about the extraordinary presence of George Peppard. Yes, the fanboy in me was already prepping to maintain composure during our art presentation. After all, the man from *Breakfast at Tiffany's* and *The Carpetbaggers* already trod on consecrated ground as far as I was concerned. Meeting him lived up to all expectations. Gracious, funny, intelligent, with a set of glacial blue eyes that I'd heretofore only ever seen twenty feet high on a movie screen, Mr. Peppard was a genuine pleasure to work with. Back to the poster design. Stylistically, I took my lead from the rubbings one makes from ancient tombstone carvings. Rather than crayon or wax, I chose to draw in charcoal and pencil to achieve a similar effect in creating this portrait of the principal characters.

MAX WOODWARD
FORMALLY VICE PRESIDENT OF THEATRE PROGRAMMING, THE KENNEDY CENTER

Ironically, excitement for a new play or musical begins with a two-dimensional visual image. The artwork represented on the window card or an ad is the first attraction before you hear the words or music or experience the excitement of live theatre.

Creating that design requires an understanding of a combination of the work's content, tone, and sensibility. Frank Verlizzo, or as we affectionately know him, Fraver, is one of the most storied and successful graphic designers on Broadway. Those of us who work in theatre know his reputation for nuance and design and interpretation. Those who simply love the theatre, know him by his work—iconic images indelibly in our minds for *Sweeney Todd*, *Deathtrap*, *The Lion King*, and so many others.

At the Kennedy Center, I had the pleasure and privilege of working with Fraver for new productions of *Little Dancer*, *Mame*, *Cat on a Hot Tin Roof,* and *The Glass Menagerie*, among others. We could always count on Fraver. His work sets the gold standard for design and it is reassuring to all of us in the theatre community to look up at the marquees and recognize yet another brilliant design by the master interpreter of theatre.

His work sells the tickets, but these brilliant designs also create the memories we all cherish of the performances that made us laugh, drew tears, or changed the way we look at love, conflict, and life. I am especially grateful for his friendship.

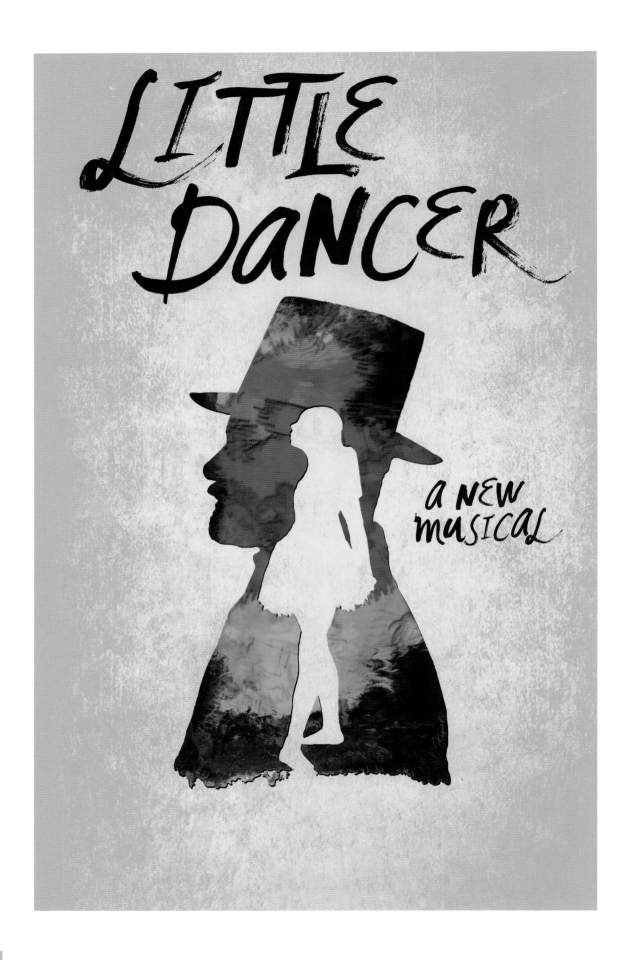

Little Dancer (2014)

Known primarily as a painter, Edgar Degas created an enduring masterpiece with his sculpture, *La Petite Danseuse de Quatorze Ans*. Over one hundred years later, it is serving as inspiration for a new musical directed and choreographed by the great Susan Stroman, with music composed by Lynn Ahrens and Stephen Flaherty. Michael Kaiser and Max Woodward of the Kennedy Center had just one request before I started designing for *Little Dancer*. They did not want to see the sculpture in the poster art. This stumped me for a while, but once I decided to concentrate on the Degas profile, the rest came easily. The figure of the young dancer is so famous, most will recognize her from her silhouette. I chose my bright colors based on the celebrated painter's brilliant palette.

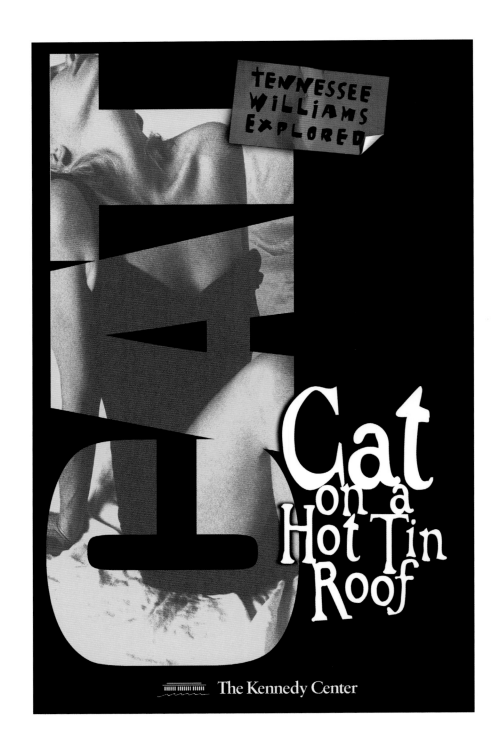

I am as big a Williams fan as I am a Sondheim fan and the Kennedy Center gave me the assignment of a lifetime, asking me to design the posters for its *Tennessee Williams Explored* celebration. Three of his greatest works: *Cat on a Hot Tin Roof*, *A Streetcar Named Desire*, and *The Glass Menagerie* were given first-class productions with amazing actors and directors. My concept, again very graphic, was to feature a famous word from each title. The word would house an image. The posters were very bold and each featured a predominant color.

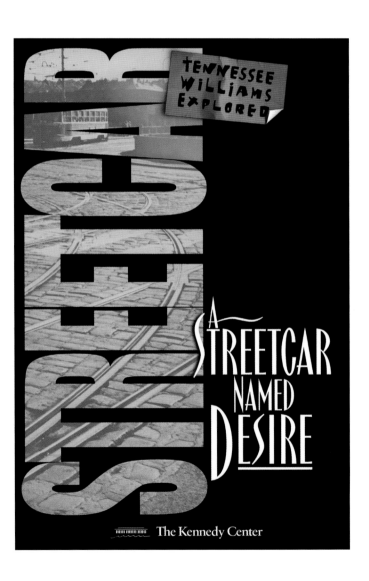

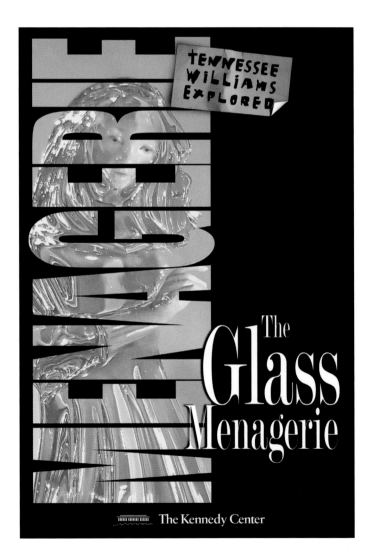

Mame (2005)

It's a daunting challenge to create a new image for a legendary show that had an equally indelible poster by Bill Berta! The Kennedy Center wanted an image completely different from Broadway's 1966 production. I started by choosing a new color palette and surrounded my Mame, Christine Baranski, with soft rose tones. The art deco illustration, my homage to artist Richard Amsel, enhanced the elegant portrait of our leading lady waving a smoky cigarette.

Side Show (2013)

It was fascinating to explore the world of carnival design in my research. The story of *Side Show* takes place in the 1930s, when most of the art was handpainted on canvas tarps or tent facades. Some were exquisite, others crude and primitive. As it turned out, I became mostly taken with the rough, gritty texture of the banner fabrics, which served to give the varied attractions a unified aura. I decided from the start that, due to the nature of Daisy and Violet's appearance, I would stay clear of anything too specific. Keeping the girls behind the canvas drape made perfect sense since no one ever saw what was behind all of those painted images at the entrance—until they paid their admittance! The poster that was chosen is a simpler version of the original, which was graphically ornamented, with illustrations of other sideshow characters.

This was a very challenging assignment from the Kennedy Center's president, Michael Kaiser, and the show's producer, Max Woodward. Challenging because, as a Pratt Institute student in the 1970s, David Edward Byrd was my illustration teacher. David designed the iconic art for the original Broadway production starring Alexis Smith, Dorothy Collins, and Yvonne DeCarlo. Having to rethink the work of my famous mentor had me in a near state of panic at first. However, once I dove into the work, I got so caught up in the many facets that shape *Follies* that my hesitations vanished. In total, I designed twelve entirely different pieces of art for this musical revival. The image that was chosen is my favorite: a theatre alley wall covered with torn, worn, and faded images of follies posters past with the negative space creating a showgirl's face. This production featured incredible A-list stars including Bernadette Peters, Jan Maxwell, and Linda Lavin.

CHAPTER SIX

UNPUBLISHED

In previous sections of this book, you've seen glimpses of some concepts and sketches for Broadway shows that were rejected for one reason or another. This last collection is probably the most exciting for me. Here is the underside of a poster presentation—the ones that didn't make it to the final printed poster. Clients in meetings were in attendance for their unveilings, but most of these designs were quickly dismissed never to be seen again. In some instances, as in *Hitchcock Blonde* (2003), the production never made the transfer from the West End to Broadway. Some shows, Anthony Newley's *Chaplin* (1983) for example, never happened at all, having closed after out-of-town tryouts. Although the full-color version I first presented is lost, you can check out my black and white comp sketch for the original Broadway production of *Into the Woods* (1987). It played bridesmaid, coming in a close second to the great poster design by Heidi Landesman ultimately chosen. There are any number of reasons why a poster falls by the wayside. Basically, it comes down to one basic cause—it just wasn't right for that production.

The obsessive fanboy in me hit new heights when it was announced that Elizabeth Taylor was coming to Broadway in *The Little Foxes* (1981). Without a thought, I picked up my pencils and began sketching. I was determined to create the poster art for my all-time favorite movie star's Broadway debut. There were just a few things wrong with that scenario: 1) The agency where I worked at the time was not handling the production's advertising and 2) Nobody asked me. After my bosses got wind of my plans, I was taken out to a lovely lunch and told that I must cease and desist. At least now, you'll have a chance to look at my initial sketch. The official Broadway poster was designed by Don Gordon, using a gorgeous photograph of Elizabeth Taylor's eyes. Who could ever compete with that anyway?

The artwork for *Victor/Victoria* was always meant to be shown as two halves on window cards and double-page ads in the *New York Times*. In 1987, when the show was originally slated to go into production, my art deco graphic was approved by Julie Andrews and Blake Edwards to represent the Broadway musical. As sometimes happens, circumstances delayed the production. When it arrived in New York City several years later, I had moved on to another agency, various producers had been added, and a photograph of the star in character was used to represent the show instead.

The story behind the unpublished art for the musical *Nick & Nora* (1991) is worth a mention. I was a big fan of *The Thin Man* noir mystery movies, but even more of a fan of the 1950s television show starring Phyllis Kirk, Peter Lawford, and their adorably sophisticated terrier, Asta. With the great pedigrees of book writer Arthur Laurents, music by Charles Strouse, and lyrics by Richard Maltby Jr., it seemed destined for musical theatre history. I was working at LeDonne & Wilner at the time and was asked to create a poster presentation expressly for the director, Mr. Laurents. Apparently, we had been awarded the show by its producers. I created six or seven posters and was instructed to head downtown to present them to Arthur Laurents at his Greenwich Village townhouse. He was extremely gracious and commented often during my presentation. When I finished, I asked him his thoughts on the art. He told me there were a few concepts he liked very much, but that I should know he wanted the advertising for the show to be handled by a rival agency and had no intention of approving any of the work I'd just shown him. I was taken aback, but since the entire process had been so pleasant, I returned to the agency to break the disappointing news. Not one to go down without a fight, my boss instructed me to create yet another art presentation for the next week. Needless to say, I was reluctant, but hey, it was *Nick & Nora* and I enjoyed designing posters for it. The next week, I went back to Mr. Laurents' place to present the new batch of artwork. Same story: he was charming, complimentary, and when the presentation was over, once again announced he had no intention of approving any of the posters for advertising. By the time I had gotten back to the office, the account had indeed moved over to the rival agency. It just would've been nice if that issue had been resolved before I'd created over twelve different designs! This poster was my favorite of the lot, but Mr. Laurents took one look at it and proclaimed, "I hate Asta!"

As for the rest, I really cannot remember the specific reasons why each of these posters didn't make the cut. I am not going to write any words of explanation in their defense. I'd like you to just enjoy looking through them with thoughts of what might have been. That, after all, is show business.

In
The

PREVIEWS BEGIN MONDAY, JANUARY 7
Prices: Mon.,Sat Eves. at 8PM, Wed. and Sat. Mats. at 2PM:Orch: $45, Mezz: $45, 35.
Mail Orders Now: Kindly list alternate dates. Mail order to "Victor/Victoria"
Times Square Station, P.O. Box 998, New York 10108

Broadway
Musical

Victor Victoria

OPENING NIGHT THURSDAY, JANUARY 17

THEATRE NAME, 444 West of Broadway, NYC

Stars of David

TOP LEFT

Pageant

BOTTOM LEFT

Bob Fosse's Big Deal

BOTTOM RIGHT

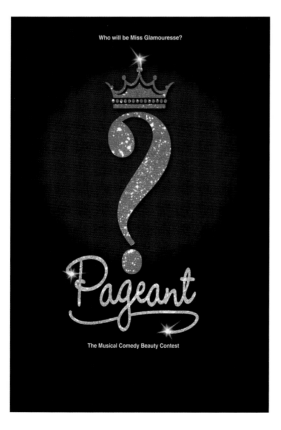

HITCH
COCK
BLONDE

Dracula

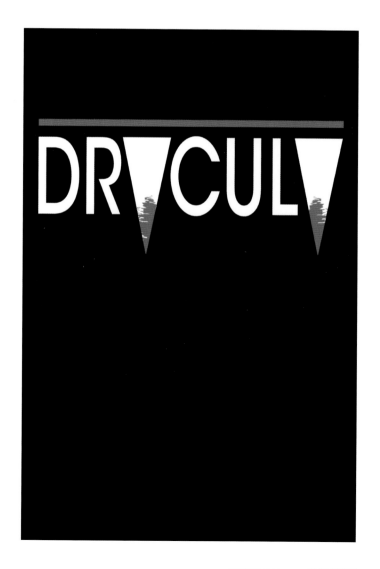

DR CUL

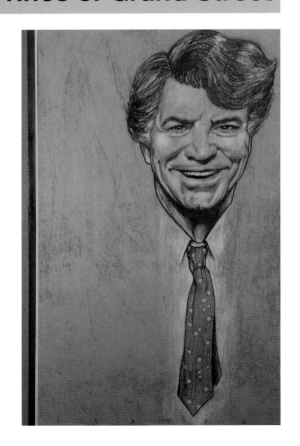

The Prince of Grand Street

The Robber Bridegroom

Home, Sweet Homer

Moose Murders

Matilda

Chaplin

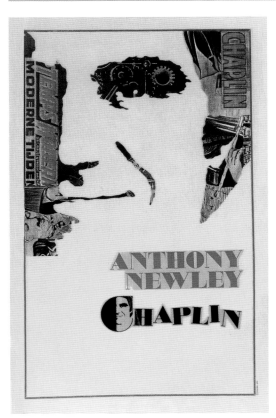

COMMENTARY
JOSEPH LIGAMMARI
MODEL, PASTRY CHEF, MUSE, AND CHEERLEADER

Frank dives into each project with excitement and enthusiasm! It starts with the script, then discussions, then an ideation phase, and finally the comps he prepares to present to the producers. For each of the more than 500 shows he's worked on in his career, he will have prepared an average of four or more concepts, which means he has designed more than 2,000 posters in the years I have known him.

My relationship to the stories in this book remind me of an Addison DeWitt quote from Joseph L. Mankiewicz's *All About Eve*, "[I am] therefore of the theatre by marriage."

I have been around the Fraver creative process for the past forty years and have witnessed the creation of great, as well as the should-have-been great, posters. I have been in the unique position of having seen them all!

Over time, I have been his biggest cheerleader and his staunchest critic. I have also been model and muse. I've had my hands photographed, my silhouette drawn, I've made wedding cakes, and posed in a tuxedo covered with Sondheim show buttons, all in the interest of art.

I can honestly say that not all of Frank's best images have been used. The producers know what best represents their show and select the poster based on that knowledge. That leaves more than seventy-five percent of the creative output unused. This section of unpublished work will give you a small sampling of the seventy-five percent. I trust you will enjoy each image as much as I have over the past five decades!

Chasing Mem'ries

Little Dancer

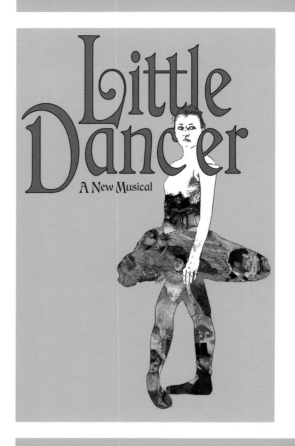

The Italian Girl in Algiers

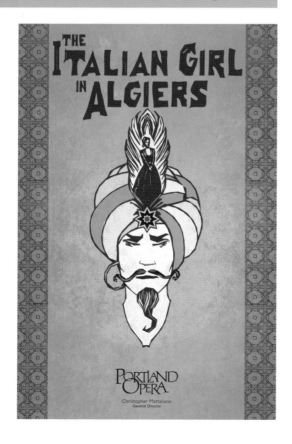

Lettice and Lovage

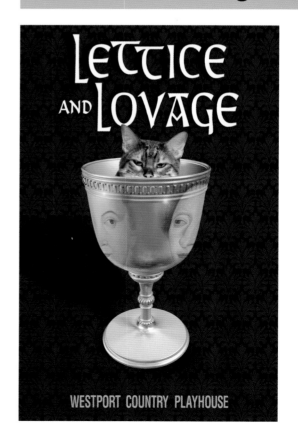

The Mountaintop

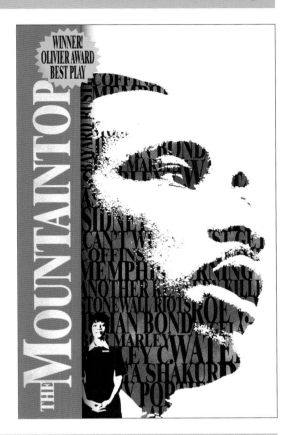

Xanadu

Marie Antoinette

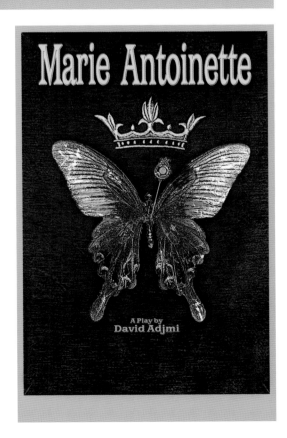

The Belle of Amherst

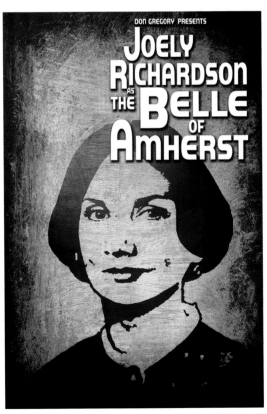

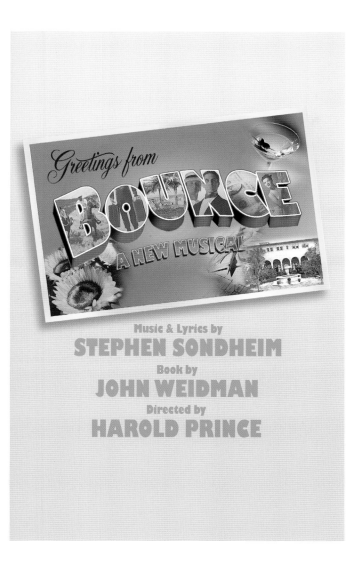

Tribes

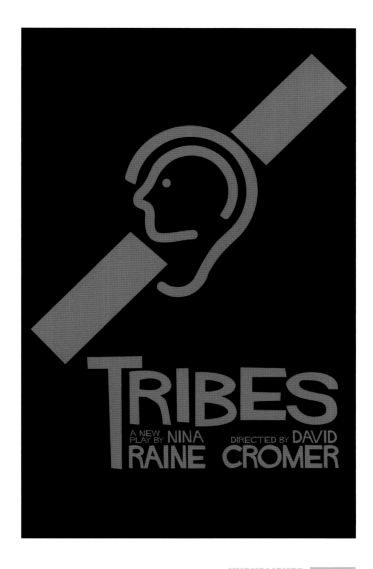

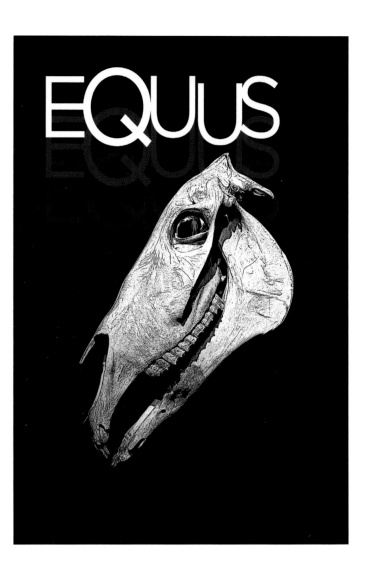

Into the Woods, Jr.

Cinderella

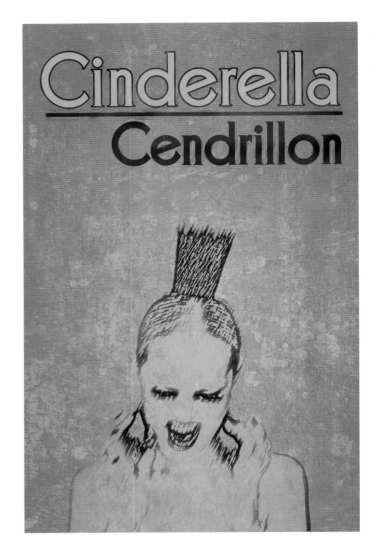

Cinderella
Cendrillon

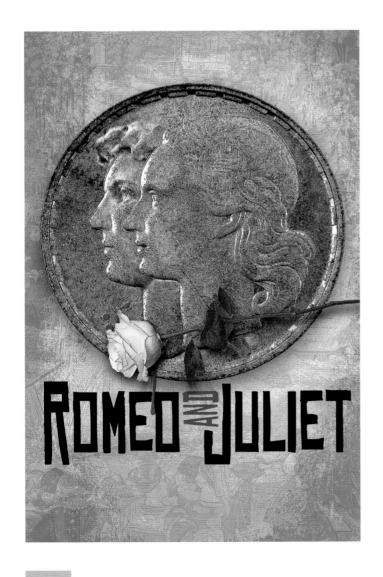

Romeo and Juliet

WHO'S WHO IN THIS BOOK

Gerard Alessandrini (Playwright, Parodist, Actor, and Stage Director) Best known for creating the award-winning Off-Broadway musical theatre parody revues *Forbidden Broadway* and *Spamilton*. Mr. Alessandrini is the recipient of Tony Honors for Excellence in Theatre, an Obie Award, four Drama Desk Awards, an Outer Critics Circle Award, and two Lucille Lortel Awards. He is also the recipient of the Drama League Award for Lifetime Achievement in Musical Theatre.

Emanuel (Manny) Azenberg (Theatre Producer and General Manager) has won numerous Tony Awards in various categories for the musicals, plays, and revivals he has presented on Broadway. His professional relationship with playwright Neil Simon spans thirty-three years. Mr. Azenberg has taught theatre at Duke University for two decades. In 2009, he was elected to the American Theatre Hall of Fame.

Rob Berman (Encores! Music Director) In 2017, Rob marked his tenth season as music director of Encores!, for which he has conducted twenty-seven productions and four cast recordings. For nine years he was music director of the Kennedy Center Honors on CBS, for which he won an Emmy Award. Mr. Berman won the Helen Hayes Award for Outstanding Musical Direction for the Kennedy Center's production of *Sunday in the Park with George*, part of the 2002 *Sondheim Celebration*.

Jon Bierman (Producer, Former Advertising Executive, and Photographer) Producing: *Finian's Rainbow* (Tony, Drama Desk, Outer Critics, Drama League nominations for Best Musical Revival), *The Gin Game*, *Love Letters*, *All About Me*. Advertising: more than 250 Broadway and Off-Broadway productions, including *Proof*, *Driving Miss Daisy*, *The Last Night of Ballyhoo*, *Journey's End*, *Thurgood*, *The Scarlet Pimpernel*, *A Doll's House*, *It Ain't Nothin' But the Blues*, and *The Glass Menagerie*. Photography: www.jonbierman.com

Jared Bradshaw (Actor and Singer) recently appeared on Broadway in the new musical *Charlie and the Chocolate Factory*. Previously, he was a long-time cast member of the Tony Award-winning smash hit *Jersey Boys*, swinging multiple roles in the Broadway, First National Tour, and Chicago companies. Off-Broadway, Jared delighted audiences in numerous incarnations of the wickedly funny *Forbidden Broadway*, deftly taking on luminaries such as Hugh Jackman, Stephen Sondheim, and John Travolta. Regional theatre highlights include: *The Music Man* (Harold Hill), *Singing in the Rain* (Don Lockwood), *Guys and Dolls* (Nathan Detroit), *Jekyll and Hyde* (Jekyll/Hyde), *West Side Story* (Riff), *Cabaret*

(Cliff), and numerous productions of *Smokey Joe's Cafe*. Additionally, he traveled as a featured performer aboard Disney Cruise Ships. Jared and wife Lindsay Northen (Broadway's *Wicked*) are the proud parents of little Georgia.

David Edward Byrd (Illustrator) created the iconic poster art for many Broadway and Off-Broadway productions, including: *Follies*, *Jesus Christ Superstar*, *Godspell*, *The Magic Show*, and *Little Shop of Horrors*. In 1973, he received a Grammy Award for album design along with several other prominent illustrators for the Who's Rock Opera, *Tommy*. From 1970 to 1979, David Byrd taught at both Pratt Institute and The School of Visual Arts. He lives in Silver Lake, Los Angeles. www.david-edward-byrd.com

Liz Callaway (Actress and Singer) is an Emmy Award-winner and Tony Award nominee for *Baby*. She made her Broadway debut in Stephen Sondheim's *Merrily We Roll Along*, and for five years played Grizabella in *Cats*. The award-winning *Sibling Revelry* (created with sister Ann Hampton Callaway) was presented to great acclaim at the Donmar Warehouse in London. She sang the Academy Award-nominated song "Journey to the Past" in the animated feature *Anastasia*. www.lizcallaway.com.

Theodore (Ted) S. Chapin (Rodgers & Hammerstein Organization) was chosen by the Rodgers and Hammerstein families to run their office. He expanded it into the Rodgers & Hammerstein Organization, which is responsible for management of the copyrights created by Richard Rodgers and/or Oscar Hammerstein II. On his watch, there have been new major productions of their musicals on Broadway (seven Tony Awards for Best Revival so far), in London, and around the world.

Jacqueline Z. Davis (Executive Director of the New York Public Library for the Performing Arts at Lincoln Center) oversees exhibitions in the center's two galleries and more than 200 programs annually, including performances and lectures. In 2011, she received the Global Interdependence Prize in New York for her work in engendering communication across cultures through the performing arts. Ms. Davis is a graduate of Harvard's Kennedy School Executive Leadership Program.

Jean Doumanian (Theatre, Television, and Film Producer) On Broadway, Jean has co-produced, and has won Tony Awards for *August: Osage County*, *The Book of Mormon*, and the 2012 revival of *Death of a Salesman*. Off-Broadway, she has co-produced the acclaimed David Cromer staging of *Our Town*, and the 2012 Drama Desk Award-winning Best Play, *Tribes*. On London's West End, she produced *The Mountaintop*, winner of the 2010 Olivier Award for Best New Play.

Bert Fink (Chief Creative Officer, Professional Licensing at Music Theatre International [MTI]) Prior to joining MTI Europe in 2016, Bert served with the Rodgers & Hammerstein Organization for more than a quarter century, most recently in London, where he was SVP/Europe and, before that, in R&H's home office in New York City. Mr. Fink began his career as a Broadway publicist, working with such theatre luminaries as Cameron Mackintosh, Andrew Lloyd Webber, and Stephen Sondheim.

Bill Haber (Theatre, Television, and Film Producer) was one of the founders of Creative Artists Agency, regarded as the most influential company in the talent agency business. He is a multiple Tony Award-winner for his Broadway stagings of: *Journey's End*, *Spamalot*, *The History Boys*, and *War Horse*. On television, Mr. Haber's Ostar Productions presents *Rizzoli & Isles* with Warner Horizon Television. In 2016, he co-produced a revival of *The Gin Game* on Broadway starring Cicely Tyson and James Earl Jones.

William Hayes (Producing Artistic Director of Palm Beach Dramaworks [PBD]) has an extensive catalogue of directing credits. A short list of his acclaimed productions at PBD includes *Exit the King*, *Picnic*, *A Delicate Balance*, and *My Old Lady*, starring Estelle Parsons. As a playwright, he is the recipient of the Charles M. Getchell Award and a member of the Dramatists Guild of America. Bill is a national ambassador for The Actors Fund.

Judy Kaye (Actress and Singer) is a two-time Tony Award winner for her featured performances in *The Phantom of the Opera* and *Nice Work If You Can Get It*. During the Broadway run of *On the Twentieth Century*, Judy made her cabaret debut at downtown's Reno Sweeney. She created the role of Emma Goldman in the Broadway production of *Ragtime*. In 2006, Ms. Kaye was nominated for the Best Actress in a Play Tony Award for *Souvenir: A Fantasia on the Life of Florence Foster Jenkins*. www.judykaye.com

Joseph Ligammari (Model, Pastry Chef, Muse, and Cheerleader) Best known as the husband of theatre poster artist Fraver, Joe can be seen on the cover of Craig Zadan's book *Sondheim & Co*, bowing on the poster for *A Life in the Theatre*, and he even baked a wedding cake for the *Company* window card as part of *The Sondheim Celebration*. While juggling his other assignments, Joe is a retired Corporate Vice President of New York Life Insurance Company.

Scott Morfee (Founding Producer of Barrow Street Theatre [BST]) is the Drama Desk award-winning producer of *Tribes*. His other critically successful Off-Broadway co-productions include *The Effect*, *Adding Machine*, *Our Town*, *Cymbeline*, *Hit the Wall*, and *Bug*. Additionally, Scott and BST have presented more than 100 shows and guest artists from around the world.

Bernadette Peters (Actress, Singer, and Children's Book Author) is one of the most critically acclaimed Broadway performers, having received two Tony Awards (plus an honorary Tony Award), three Drama Desk Awards, an Outer Critics Circle Award, and a Golden Globe Award. She is widely considered to be the premier interpreter of Stephen Sondheim's work with *Sunday in the Park with George*, *Into the Woods*, *A Little Night Music*, and *Follies* to her credit. Ms. Peters and Mary Tyler Moore co-founded Broadway Barks, an annual animal adopt-a-thon held in New York City. She has also written two children's books with the proceeds benefitting Broadway Barks: *Broadway Barks* (Blue Apple Books, 2008), *Stella Is a Star* (Blue Apple Books, 2010), and *Stella and Charlie, Friends Forever* (Blue Apple Books, 2015).

Dean Pitchford (Songwriter, Screenwriter, Director, Actor, and Novelist) His work has earned him a Best Song Oscar and a Golden Globe Award for the title song "Fame." Mr. Pitchford wrote the lyrics for the stage musical of *Carrie*. The musical stage adaptation of his original screenplay for *Footloose* ran for more than 700 performances on Broadway and is now seen all over the world. Dean's middle-grade novels, *The Big One-Oh* and *Captain Nobody*, are published by Putnam/Penguin. His third novel, *Nickel Bay Nick*, was published to acclaim (Penguin Young Readers Group, 2013) www.deanpitchford.com

Susan L. Schulman (Theatrical Press Agent) has handled Broadway and Off-Broadway plays, musicals, and not-for-profit art institutions for more than forty years. A native New Yorker, she began as a "theatre kid" who hung around stage doors. Her many Broadway productions include Bob Fosse's *Dancin'*, *Dream*, *State Fair*, *Applause*, *Sly Fox*, *Death of a Salesman*, *Death and the Maiden*, *A Streetcar Named Desire*, and *Requiem for a Heavyweight*. She is the author of the book *Backstage Pass to Broadway: More True Tales from a Theatre Press Agent* (Goodreads Press, 2017) www.BackstagePassToBroadway.com.

Claudia Shear (Playwright and Actress) first came to prominence with her acclaimed solo performance piece *Blown Sideways Through Life*. She wrote and starred in the play *Dirty Blonde*, her exploration of the life and career of Mae West. Ms. Shear earned Tony and Drama Desk Award nominations for both Best Play and Best Actress and won the Theatre World Award. Her play *Restoration* premiered Off-Broadway at New York Theatre Workshop in 2010. She co-wrote the book for the musical *Tuck Everlasting*, which opened on Broadway in 2016.

Jack Viertel (Encores! Artistic Director) has been in charge of Encores! since 2000, overseeing fifty-one productions and counting. He is also senior vice president of Jujamcyn Theaters. He conceived and co-produced the long-running musical revue *Smokey Joe's Cafe*. He was a producer of the Broadway revival of *Gypsy* starring Patti LuPone, which was first seen at Encores! Summer Stars in 2007. Mr. Viertel's new book is *The Secret Life of the American Musical* (Farrar, Straus, and Giroux, 2016).

Max Woodward (Formerly Vice President of Theatre Programming at The John F. Kennedy Center for the Performing Arts in Washington, D.C.), recently retired, had been with the organization since the complex's opening in 1971. Mr. Woodward oversaw the facility's operation but later became the supervisor of all the theatre programming and much of the in-house production. He produced some of the Kennedy Center's best original ventures during Michael Kaiser's tenure as president, including the landmark event *Sondheim Celebration* in 2002 and *Tennessee Williams Explored* in 2004. Max has an extensive theatre poster collection.

INDEX